I0756622

HUMBLE ANECDOTES

—— OF THE ——

INVISIBLE

KEN EVANS

authorHOUSE®

AuthorHouse™ UK
1663 Liberty Drive
Bloomington, IN 47403 USA
www.authorhouse.co.uk
Phone: 0800 047 8203 (Domestic TFN)
        +44 1908 723714 (International)

Published by AuthorHouse 08/28/2019

ISBN: 978-1-7283-9247-9 (sc)
ISBN: 978-1-7283-9246-2 (e)

INTRODUCTION

'Humble Anecdotes of the Invisible' is the final part of my condensed Lebenswelt Studies. Necessarily autobiographical, and centred mostly on what amounted to a 'mesocosm' — an *intermediary spiritual -world,* between the macrocosm and microcosm, by artists, thinkers, poets and dancers who founded an experimental community, the 'Hill of Truth' in Ascona, during the early onset of Modernism, and later at Eronos the intellectual and aesthetic hub founded by Olga Frobe in Ascona in 1933, to discuss the most pressing issues of the times: the nature of body and soul, social norms, religious belief, relationships, value of life, the human spirit, art and creativity; and their eventual making of an alternative spiritual and intellectual history of the twentieth century.

Ken Evans combines his academic and professional interests working as a university lecturer in social sciences and philosophy, and as a Consultant to statutory and private Care Providers in mental health, elderly care, and international care education and training. His on-going research interests are in combining and integrating theoretical perspectives from all fields of 'human traditions and categories' in the application of health and social care.

THE VISIBLE AND THE INVISIBLE

The coupling of the two words *visible* and *invisible* would most probably be either meaningless or a conundrum to most of the present generation; but for the older generation, the one I grew up in, it would almost certainly mean a distinction between two worlds, the physical and the metaphysical or the 'material' and the mytho-poetical (spiritual).The most obvious consequences of this difference between generations would be in how we each make sense of our 'lifeworlds'; that is how we understand and see ourselves, and how we relate to one another, and how we use language; in other words the *measure* of our cultural capital and our civility.

Sociologically speaking, the socially constructed *meanings* we make of both the visible and invisible worlds are historically and geographically contextualised, changing over time and space! In our modern digitalised world we commonly use *data to make our point,* as a kind of *shorthand,* as if it is possible to explain everything by numbers; but frequently in the past we used poetry and stories, mostly in the form of *anecdotes;* presenting reflexive accounts of real-life experiences, condensed and homogenised, and in some sense necessarily anonymous. Hence it is easy for any one of us to see ourselves within stories told to us, as perhaps, for example even as; "That *certain man* (who) went down from Jerusalem to Jericho", etc. We use anecdotes as a shorthand means of making our point. Anecdotes are universal across all cultures and times, especially when defining the style of sacred and mythopoetic literature, and partly for this reason they frequently pop-up in my own student-lectures!

On a recent visit to Rome I was reminded once more of the literal origin of the *anecdote*. Although Diogenes is casually credited with popularising the use of his 'brief pithy stories' to illustrate his complex philosophical thoughts, the real originator of the anecdote is Procopius of Caesarea, a Private Secretary, cum Advisor to Belisarius who was Emperor Justinian's Byzantine's Army General.

Procopius accompanied Belisarius during his campaigns in Africa and Italy, and wrote a much applauded 'A History of the Wars', and whilst collecting his material for this, he picked-up inside information (Court gossip) about his boss the General, and about the General's wife and also about the hidden goings-on in the royal court, which he titled; *'Anecdota',* better known to historians as *'The Secret History',* in other words *his* secret history revealing what otherwise would or should have remained hidden. For me this is the most important characteristic of anecdotes; the making *visible* of what otherwise might have remained *invisible;*

hidden or unseen. Indeed I would go further to claim this is one of its defining essences making stories so vital to public understanding, and everyday communication.

Some time ago, during the lean years of my teaching, when I was introducing fresh undergraduates to philosophy, I became known for my (apparently annoying) habit when responding to student's questions during my lectures; when I would reply to them, asking if they preferred either a 'short answer or an interesting one'! They soon came to understand that the choice between the barest of bones of an explanation or a well-padded explication, frequently involved an extensive detour for a convoluted anecdote, perhaps, including warts and all! In other words something to 'hammer-home' what I considered to be essential points!

I suppose after a while this became my style, and to some extent still is; even now when dealing with ordinary domestic matters across the family dining table; and I suppose very oddly, even when responding to anonymous telephone calls from Call-Centres. Everyone gets the full-works, which is intended to irritate the Call-Centre callers as much as their calls irritate me! I have to admit I cannot resist any opportunity to share my weakness for anecdotes!

Which brings me to my main point. That *anecdotes* remain under-valued, especially as a literary device, besides being seen perhaps as threateningly subversive, and even inferior to so-called *facts*, especially in academic disputation. Recalling my own student days of essay writing, and being told by my Poitics Lecturer that my essays were more like 'journalism' because of my preference for *anecdotal evidence*. Poor old

George S. (in the Politics Department), whose only delight seemed to have been dubbing my essays with large red ink 'Cs', because of *insufficient facts*. In my mind's eye I see him now, squirming behind his desk, readjusting his taupe and banging his eyes at me, and mouthing something along the lines of the words from Charles Dickens 'Hard Times'. 'Now, what I want (Evans) is, Facts. . . You can only form the minds of reasoning animals upon Facts: Stick to Facts, Evans!'. Sadly his remonstrations only made matters worse; to the point when he eventually became one of my anecdotes!

Being revisited by anecdotes from the past is fast becoming a habit of mine: when I wake early in the morning with fragments of dreams floating round in my head, requiring fitting evasive anecdotes into meaningful narratives, sometimes my mind pursues odd questions, which could just as quickly fizzle-out, or perhaps take-up residence deeply in my unconscious mind chasing other fleeting thoughts, or sometimes resting and returning when temporarily they think they might have found somewhere to stay. I think this was how it was for Merleau-Ponty, when nearing the end of his life, outlining his thoughts for what would have been his final publishable work, now known as 'The Visible and Invisible', which tantalisingly left more unanswered questions than possible answers. Some wild responses from his followers suggested some sort of 'intellectual disappointment,' as if in some sense the final thoughts of a life-long philosopher should have revealed profound metaphysical insights! What they should have realised is that even the profoundest philosophical writers are in the same boat as the rest of us when it comes to understanding the 'invisible', and that they might have been better-off sticking with the 'visible' by simply reading more poetry!

Generally, only poets stand any chance of shedding light on the realm of the *invisible*, which for most of us we can only ponder! I have been, and still am, a student of Philosophy as well as Sociology, and sit uncomfortably somewhere in between. For me any answers to any question should meet the peculiar demands of both heart and mind (soul), and of course our reflexive imagination. I was contemplating these sorts of questions before getting out of bed one recent morning, and as it was snowing hard outside, the room still cold, I decided to wait while the central heating boiler came-on to warm-up the house, and in the meantime listened to BBC radio 'Four', 'Desert Island Discs'; a mildly passive physical activity of listening; offering insights into what might otherwise remained *invisible*.

The thoughts and feelings of the castaway that morning, Wendy Cope, a poet who communicated her life-long 'invisible thoughts and feelings' via her choice of eight gramophone recordings; what could be simpler and easier than this in gaining access to some small part of the invisible? Besides this single example, I learned also that the BBC has an archive of a further two thousand castaway editions, of which this one is what sociologists might deem an 'opportunistic sample', randomly selected by the randomness of a cold bedroom! Actually I nearly de-randomised it by switching off the radio half way through the second chosen record - Gilbert and Sullivan's 'Tit Willow'. But again the randomness of the following

Mozart's Duet from 'The Magic Flute', stayed my finger on the on/off button, followed by 'Coulter's Candy', and again my arm shot-out to silence the radio; yet again I faltered!

It wasn't so much, the rather whimsical assortment of music which was holding my attention, as the nature of Wendy Cope's reminiscences; brilliantly inter-woven anecdotes of her life, through and around her choice of musical illustrations, revealing the highs and lows of her relations with her parents (especially her mother), depression and therapy, then discovery that she could write good poetry. That is why I heard her out, through to the final record, the carefully chosen; Bach's Church Cantata, 'Watchet auf, ruft uns die Stimme', also known as the hymn, 'Sleepers Awake'; a piece full of hidden anecdotes!

It was this final choice of music that stunned me into returning to thinking about my own essay on the 'visible and invisible', more so because of her choice of the unusual version by a 'Mandolin, Cello and Bass Ensemble,' (Yo-Yo Me, Chris Thile and Edgar Meyer), which somehow sharpened the haunting counterpoint, like the frenetic cry of the Watchman; 'Awake, Awake'; hanging in the air as if to confirm Wendy Cope's fondness of hymns and her own sense of urgency. She had mentioned that she liked hymn tunes at the start of the interview, which she explained by reference to her experience of Boarding School Morning Assemblies, and her mother's 'peculiar' religiosity, which included attendances at Billy Graham Rallies; she being the one to 'Come Forward'! I was rapidly beginning to understand the agony of her relationship with both mother and religion, and also the roots of her Depression!

As I lay listening and thinking about her story, my now wakening unconscious mind was empathising with the words,'Flying' like the night, in Philipp Nicolais's opening line of the chorale; 'Wake, Awake, For Night is Flying'; I felt the urgency of her life-long panic, and was sure she must have been familiar with the parable of the Ten Virgins; at some time perhaps even identifying with those waiting, unprepared for some momentous event!

If all of this sounds cryptic it is because it has to be! For perhaps we are all at some time in our lives *foolish virgins*. The meaning of which becomes clearly visible in the parable of the Ten Virgins story, as referred to in St.Mathew's Gospel, Chapter 25, Verses 1-13., an anecdote almost, which gives only the barest bones of the story in the hymn and the music I had been listening to. For behind this combination of words and music were deeper layers of the cantata's urgent message, as experienced by Philipp Nicolai, a sixteenth century German priest poet and the original composer of the words and melody of the hymn; who experienced both the cruel upheaval of the Reformation as well as suffering the misery of the Great Plague, with which I am sure Wendy Cope had already, in part identified, in her own way as perhaps one poet to another? Catching his sense of urgency to be ready, not to miss 'the momentous Wedding Feast' celebrating the *invisible* marriage, of Jesus the mystical Bridegroom, as well as to the 'Souls of Humanity'. Music unmistakably and unforgettably adapted later, and harmonised by

J.S.Bach, like a persistent remembered melody from my own school-day's morning Assemblies, and even probably shared at that very moment by many other listeners of my own generation, who might have been listening then to that radio programme, some perhaps like me, lying in the warm comfort of their beds, their minds and souls like mine, reminiscing and wondering about their own distant memories of school Morning Assemblies.

My own fleeting memories of Assemblies were part of yet a bigger picture at that time, mainly of the desolate years during and after the War, and my family's feelings of recovering from even worse times; but I remember above all the strange effects of singing hymns; stirring melodies and bold poetical words burning their incandescent images into my boyish imagination, which strangely at the time I failed to connect with further stories from Scripture lessons which followed Assemblies, which I realise only now, all the time had been quietly nurturing my interior life.

Stranger still was my own secret discovery of the hidden power of those extraordinary words, which to my boyish way of thinking had been smuggled into school hymns, not to be sung and then forgotten after we had left the school hall, but to be carried away by me to my classroom, to be remembered and repeated to myself secretly during less interesting lessons, over and over again like magical mantras that would embolden me with *invisible* strengths, and make my imagination fly with images of the *Voice of God* 'speaking through 'Earthquakes, Wind and Fire'! (Such was the oddness of my beliefs at that time!)

It never occurred to me in those times that this was some rare experience for my little soul, as it must have been for all men of many generations before my own. I'm now thinking back to an earlier discussion in another of my books (The Homely Mind), of an event, of one generation's experience of the First Wold War, and one particular haunting image of soldiers, ordinary fathers and sons, captured on a primitive movie camera at the actual moment of 'going over the top' from their trenches, running across no-man's land towards their enemy, against a relentless hail of machine-gun bullets. One particular young boyish face remaining fixed in my mind's eye; dazed and frozen with fear, standing out from the others, and yet each and every one of them knowingly locked into a shared uncompromising *moment* of having to face an unseen (invisible) enemy, clumsily scrambling out of their trenches to meet their almost certain instant death!

Bach's Cantata No.140 captures all of the compressed energy of such urgent moments, from the moment of the arrival of the Bridegroom at the Wedding Feast, to the ecstatic moment for men about to meet their instant death on the battle-field.

I discovered that this moment was also seen as a turning point in the history of the Church of England, according to Alan Watkinson, (The Church of England and the First World War.1996, p.p. 248,) It seems that; "The Church of England had lost its hold on the nation; after sixteen centuries of influence", . . .The tide is ebbing within and without the Churches. The drift is towards a non-dogmatic affirmation of general kindliness and good fellowship, with an emphasis rather on the service of men than the fulfilment of the will of God. . . *It is the passing of a whole civilisation away from faith in which it was founded and out of which it has been fashioned."*

Watkinson's book, a densely written account of the role of the Church of England, both in the Foreign Field and Home Front during the First World War, with representative voices from within and without the Church; for example:

"C.E.Montague, enlisting in his late forties. He served in the army during the whole of the war. He was on the staff of the *Manchester Guardian* for thirty-five years. His reflection of the war with the representative title *Disenchantment* published in 1922, written in the belles-lettres style. His attitude to the Church was critical and rather lofty. In his chapter, 'The sheep were not Fed', he gave voice to his conviction that the Church had had a great opportunity among the soldiers, but was incapable of seizing it. A soldier might be six months in France before a religious service came his way.'(p.p.117)

Although this book cites anecdotes of individual army chaplain's acts of courage and pastoral care in the field, the main criticism was that there was no ecclesiastical or theological leadership in the role of the Nation's Church in the face of a war of this magnitude, with such massive loss of life. Not only were the sheep not fed, but the shepherds were scattered! "Lord Parmoor, the Archbishop of Canterbury's Vicar General, wrote in October1914: 'Each day the weakening influence of Christianity becomes clearer', he went on to say that the Churches instead of preaching the

Gospel of peace were encouraging an opportunist war spirit because it was popular, and so were losing their real (spiritual) power."

It should have been self-evident to senior Churchmen that the nation's Church had long failed it's people, socially and politically; it being identified in the popular mind as more a *middle-class* institutional thing, insufficiently applying the Christian message to social questions, to the extent that the working classes had come to see themselves as outsiders; never to be invited to the 'Banquet'- of *Weddings,* or otherwise! For the average Tommy felt that the C of E had long before, turned its back on them in spiritual matters; their natural response was to revert back to some instinctual deeper-rooted traditional folk beliefs; to anecdotes of prophecies, spirits, magic, and protective talismans, as outlined in Owen Davies thesis, 'A Supernatural War' (2018 OUP), whose central point broadly speaking, was that where ordinary soldier's and their family's spiritual needs were not being met by their national church, particularly so during the war, they sought solace in alternative sources of spiritual help, especially in various forms of *spiritualism.*

Yet Tommy's response to his own fears was that there is 'Something', that might be instinctual, and timeless, and fundamentally human; that indefinable 'feeling' or 'sensation' that there really is a 'Something', which almost certainly for the average Tommy, would have been beyond his comprehension or ability to explain. I understand that this 'Something' they felt in those 'circumstances', especially in those extreme living conditions of the trenches in the battle-field, must have been a sense of the *numinous;* a believable hint of the *invisible* spiritual world, and that in that instance of preparing to clamber over the top, each Tommy's intimations were more towards his own almost immediate mortality, than his immortality!

As Davies contends;

"Numerous strange visions and sensations experienced by soldiers and their loved ones were reported during the war, and were described variously at the time as 'the uncanny under fire' or 'war and the weird'. Wars have always generated stories (anecdotes) of apparitions, ghostly encounters, and strange premonitions, but there had never before been such a keen interest in the supernatural or otherworldly experiences of the military as during and after the Great War."

Davies believes; "This was due, in large part, to the extraordinary early twentieth-century convergence of scientific and religious interest in metaphysics and the esoteric respectively, coupled with a general-public ever receptive to *proofs of a spiritual side to life.* And the key to understanding much of this rapprochement with the supernatural, and how it has been interpreted since, now lies in our understanding of the spiritualist movement." (2018 Davies, p.p.54)

There were 'Heavenly signs and Visitations, Haunted Landscapes, Spirits on the Battlefield, Premonitions, Fortune Telling, Magical Services, Lucky Charms, Talismans, Seances, and all manner of means of warding off evil."

Even Sigmund Freud investigated the country-wide increase in the use of psychics and clairvoyants after the First World War, as families and loved ones attempted to contact their dead fathers and sons who had died on the battle-fields. Freud attributed this rapidly growing interest in occult practices as a response to the collapse in traditional values and 'total loss of value'!

Church leaders were well aware of these activities and tried to avert them, but it seemed that Tommy preferred his own means of connecting with the *invisible* spirit world through his own *anecdotal* knowledge. Shared with his comrades through the everyday transmission of news and stories, mostly anecdotes, passed on from one soldier to another, one family and another. Such an ordinary matter of fact, one might say; part of everyday life, whether in the trenches or at home in the workplace, for the sharing of anecdotes was and is, so mundanely part of life that they are hardly noticed, and strangely that they would, in a sense, remain a *mystery* to the Church authorities, and how they might combat what they considered a 'superstitious' threat to their 'religious authority'.

And yet if the Churchmen had considered this further, and perhaps thought about how ideas and beliefs are transmitted from one individual to another, they might also have pondered how this might also have happened at the earliest beginnings of their own faith, at the time even of the original roots of Christianity itself, when communication was only by word of mouth, through the medium of unconnected anecdotes; (not that they were called this at that time). But anecdotes they were; indeed the whole Bible, both New and Old, is composed entirely of anecdotes, as are all the major works of Homer and Virgil, even Plato's Symposium, and all other great human myths which underwrite religious thinking.

The next leap of my imagination carried me to thinking about our own personal cognitive beginnings, about how any of us learn anything, and the growth of our own social understanding; which sociologists and psychologists refer to as 'Primary Socialisation'. Our earliest experiences and events enabling us to become social members of society, through acquiring language and the social norms of our culture, firstly through our family and peers, and then through school and other grouping. At this stage of our lives these are the main socialising agents, but the means of transmission is through the things we say to one another; explanations and examples via *little stories* we tell ourselves and one another, in other words *anecdotes*. And we ourselves recreate these stories through our imaginations, inventing and adapting them, and in some sense re-living our own primary socialisation through our children; this is why, for the same reasons, School Assembly hymns sung so many years ago still stick in our minds.

Hymn-singing in every morning assembly, at the start of the school-day, created for me something akin to a mental and emotional map; new magical words to my ears, burning images deeply into my imagination, of God's invisible world conjuring-up believable pictures in ways that nothing else would or could have! Words such as; *'Great Father of Glory, pure Father of Light'* (407); His army of saints, *'Ten thousand times ten thousand, in sparkling raiment bright' (486),* 'Whose arm *doth bind the restless wave'* (540) and many more epithets becoming part of my own secret language. Only much later did I realise that these phrases were anecdotal pointers to deeper philosophical and theological questions; as is the case of Wendy Cope's chosen hymn, which tells a story in human terms; "Wake, O wake, with tidings thrilling. The watchmen all the air are filling, Arise, Jerusalem, arise! Midnight strikes! No more delaying, 'The Hour has come!' We hear them saying. Where are ye all, ye virgins wise? Raise high your torches bright! The Bridegroom comes in sight." These words based on the parable of Ten Virgins, in chapter 25 of Mathew's Gospel; "Then shall the kingdom of heaven be likened unto ten virgins, which took their lamps and went forth to meet the bridegroom".

But deeper still; to one of the earliest Christian mystics; Origen (c.184-238). Here the quality of the language becomes richer; more intricate and poetically intimate. [The adjective *mystical* in the original Greek means 'hidden'] Origen, in his Prologue to Commentary on the 'Song of Songs', connects Mathew's *parable of the virgins* with Solomon's erotic 'Song of Songs', which he describes as an epithalamium, (that is to say a marriage song), as an account of the bridegroom and bride, as the story of the love between Christ (the bridegroom) and His bride the church; but he furthered the meaning of this mystical reading by applying it to the relations between Christ and each loving soul'; which is how it is now commonly understood.

Yet all our delving through layers of meaning rests on our own 'basic assumptions' for the existence or reality of God; not even necessarily a loving God, but for a God *plain and simple*; for a God we actually believe to exist! I realise now that this *seemed* to be the 'crunch' question, but not quite; for when the words of another hymn; *'Through the night of doubt and sorrow'*, drifts into my mind, I take theses words to mean doubts about the existence of God, until at some further point, my focus of concern switches; becoming more the doubts about the claims of our political institution's 'God' of the Churches, 'a social construct' beginning with the Emperor Constantine's adoption of Christianity, as Rome's 'official' religion. The real reasons for this are still obscure, but whatever the case, it seems to have set the pattern for the history of 'national institutional churches' throughout Europe, even up to the present day, which is to say not for *spiritual* reasons, but for *political* reasons, rather than because of the authenticity of the Christian's claims for the divinity of Jesus. From the earliest days, Constantine's recognition of Christianity as the official state religion, the Church became a political instrument, dedicated to the destruction of so-called paganism; actually destroying temples to the old gods and replacing them with Christian church buildings, usually on the same site!

And once Christianity became dominant, it dominated; setting the civilising agenda for the whole of Europe; right up to the present day. When to speak of Western Culture; of its languages, philosophy, arts, laws, its myths, it's values, and so-forth, in essence is to speak of Christian Culture, which held the Roman inheritance together right up to the Reformation; when institutional greed and corruption challenged the hegemony of the singular Catholic organisation, out of which Henry VIII, King of England grabbing its wealth and possessions in his patch, declaring himself 'Supreme Leader of the Church in England'. That also is why our present monarch is the head of the National Church, and why British Prime Misters, as Head of British Governments select our Archbishops, and that is why the C of E is still 'Institutionalised', and why I have difficulties believing that any God worth His *salt*, would be willing to operate exclusively through this politically contrived Institutional Organisation, that has all the trimmings of a franchised Business enterprise!

I'm now visualising (visiting) a fictionalised C of E's Organisation's chart, perhaps hanging somewhere, on the wall in the PM's office or in Buckingham Palace, showing God (perhaps in a heavenly cloud) at its apex, and immediately below, the Monarch (its Supreme Governor on Earth), and thirdly the Archbishop of Canterbury, (House of Lords & Lambeth Palace) all displaying its Mission Statement, from the Book of Common Prayer, as:

"The Visible Church of Christ is a congregation of faithful men, in which the pure Word of God is preached, and the sacraments be duly ministered according to Christ's ordinance in all those things that of necessity are requisite to the same. The British monarch has the constitutional title of Supreme Governor of the Church of England. The canon law of the Church of England states, "We acknowledge that the Queen's most excellent Majesty, acting according to the laws of the realm, is the *highest power under God in this kingdom,* (I'm assuming God is OK about this arrangement?) has supreme authority over all persons in all causes, as well ecclesiastical as civil. In practice this power is often exercised through Parliament and the Prime Minister. In England and Wales, the Archbishop of Canterbury is the highest in precedence following the royal family. His only theological qualification for his current position is that at the age of 19 he began speaking in tongues, and continues to do so! This is the Visible Church spoken for, but what of the Invisible Church and the intimate relationship between God and individual members of that Church since the beginning of Christianity? Certainly some, perhaps most of the Tommies during the First World War would have been signed-up from birth; as casual attenders, others, non-attending - nominally members, and the remainders, assumed to be 'foolish virgins'. And much earlier still, after the Reformation, most definitely Philipp Nicholai's name would be high on the membership list, he was after all a priest, a poet, and a Mystic, therefore a highly *committed* participant in both the Visible and the Invisible Church; as such he would have dedicated himself to an in-depth engagement with God, "through prayer, contemplation and deep reading of biblical text; delighting in *multiple* meanings and illuminating one biblical text with another' (McGinn 2006).

Retracing my own academic routes back through philosophy and sociology, it has long puzzled me that academic sociology has produced remarkably little in way of explaining how religious beliefs shape individual and community lives; sociological studies stop short at explaining how bible stories shape lives. Perhaps researchers would find it too difficult to intrude in such personal experiences of individual's relationship with their God! For example what kinds of questions would they ask, and how would they decipher responses? I am also sure that some responses would be interpreted as irrational, and perhaps even mad. Especially within our Post-Modernised frames of reference, in which there would be embarrassment in using biblical language (except for the occasional evangelicals who knock on my door). To read accounts of mystics, such as Origen and Gregory of Nyssa is the closest *experience* to reading anthropological accounts of rare, almost extinct, Amazonian tribal-people. But these mystical accounts are very worthwhile reading, if for no other reason than to learn how common and uncommon Christian beliefs reflected the times in which they were written, and 'world-views' of their congregations.

Philipp Nicholai (1575-1597) lived in dangerous theological times, when individuals and countries went to war over their theological squabbles. (The ordinary Tommies of those times survived by following their leaders; not so very different from Tommies fighting in the Great War trenches!) But Nicholai was far from being a foot-soldier of the church; for as a Priest, Poet and Mystical thinker, Hymn Composer, with a Doctorate of Divinity Degree, and a clear vision of Christian commitment, he would have been regarded as a Christian Leader, as someone influencing his Flock, his Parishioners; and still influencing worshippers today in the way in which his hymns and music reinforces the strong notes of 'joy and adoration', distinguishing his hymns with their mystical undertones, as distinctively different from many others in the Lutheran tradition.

He also strongly argued against the Catholic Counter-Reformation, by his appeal for the 'essential nature of God', and 'the reality of the incarnation, the truth of atonement, the kingly rule of the incarnate Word, the accessibility of the Grace of the Holy Spirit in the Word of God, and his deep commitment to a doctrine of the joyful Mystical Union of Christ and the Believers, as the Celestial bridegroom, and of life everlasting.

I now imagine were he to suddenly reappear in any C of E pulpit, shouting "Awake, O Awake", he would most likely be Sectioned, under the Mental Health Act! Such is the Way of All Flesh in these Modern Times, and the anaemic bloodless and insipid message of the post modern and almost post-Christian Church of England. What happened to the *Mystical*, (mystical meaning *hidden* in Greek)? Where has the subtle poetry of theological disputation gone, where also the common belief in the *Soul,* and of 'all things visible and invisible?

I'm not asking these questions as a priest or a preacher, but as a Sociologist; whose main interest is the nature of Modern Society with it's concerns for a *visibly* equal value and quality of life for all citizens; and for the loss of community and why the C of E's (our national church) pews are emptying, it's congregations being forced to look elsewhere for the *invisible,* with which to nurture their own souls, but I sympathise with our Cof E parish clergy when I take an occasional peep inside local churches, to observe the official Church's tedium, which for some, it's *main* business of 'saving souls', now seeming to be an empty occupation, especially difficult in times when nobody understands biblical language anymore or it's meandering narratives. In fact I go further still, in no longer understanding what the Church means by 'worship', or whether an invisible God really needs it? Or whether there is still any connection with Nicholai's declared beliefs in the; reality of the incarnation, atonement, and the mystical union of Christ and His Followers. Should we not take and try to understand one anecdote at a time?

Anecdotes are like small interludes in a wider narrative, linking ideas together, their effectiveness resting on their ability to literally add 'flesh' and energy to the bare bones of a story, by bringing in 'extras' as in a film scene. They are the leavening agent, revealing a common truth by adding personal details and making incidents come alive; setting the social context as well as adding depth, colour and atmosphere; as if inviting listeners or readers, physically into the picture; drawing them into the scene, more like participants than simply onlookers, using their own imagination and emotions, giving the example credibility. In fact it is this reflexive quality (the possibility of putting ourselves into the other's situation) of anecdotes which is the source of their hidden power. The more I think about the character of anecdotes the more convinced I am that they are, and have been for centuries, the vitalising power of all major historical narratives and the means of humanising them. I am surprised that no-one-else seems to have noticed this!

Most daily anecdotes are so routine that they aren't worth the re-telling, but some exceptional anecdotes can expand in the telling. For example, recently when I attempted to explain in an article I had been writing for publication, an anecdote of my embarrassment of disingenuousness, I found the necessity of describing the context, which required considerable amplification almost to the point of losing my central point! And the point was quite simply, that one cannot always be *true to oneself*!

This anecdote referred to a real experience. One evening in my wife's village in Northern Luzon, in the Philippines, where not much ever seems to happen! But one late evening as I was wandering along the road, searching for the giant croaking frogs filling the otherwise silence with their loud noises, I was suddenly apprehended by a posse of small children asking me if I wanted to see a 'dead woman'. We couldn't understand one another, but they insisted I come with them. They led me back along to where I had already walked, to a house where there seemed to be some sort of gambling party going on, for the entire front yard was lit-up with strings of fairy-lights, with groups of young people sitting around tables diligently playing card games. I was led by the children to the front-door of the house without the slightest idea what was happening.

The door opened and I was invited in by two very elderly women and shown to one of the empty chairs arranged against the four sides of the room, and sat down, still having no idea what it was all about. The other elderly people seemed to be acknowledging me as if they knew who I was, although I couldn't recognise any of them; then it occurred to me that it might be a 'Wake' or something, but it still didn't make sense that in front of the house many young people were apparently enjoying themselves!

After a while a very elderly man wearing a white Barong Tagalog (Filipino shirt) came from another door and thanked me for coming, and took my hand and led me back into his darkened room, unlit except for two giant-sized candles, one either end of a small white coffin standing on trestles.

He squeezed my hand and whispered; "That's my wife.... married for fifty-five years. . . she died!"

He led me to the coffin, which had a plate-glass lid, and motioned that I should look in. Lying deep inside was the smallest child-sized body of his wife! Tears were welling-up in his eyes, his expression vacant, his pain obvious! Then gripping my hand tightly, he explained,. . . I was the Methodist Pastor here in this place, . . . I grew up here, . . . I was trained by Methodists Missionaries from America, . . . and returned here to be their Pastor, . . . here among my congregation. He looked at his dead wife and then directly into my eyes as if questioning me, searching my face for an answer without a question. His body shaking with pain and anguish!

"All I want to know is," He faltered for a moment, then again, he asked. "All I want to know, . . is, . . will I see my wife again?"

He was still peering at me, silently prodding me for a reply, all the other mourners watching us as if expecting me to do something, I could sense that they knew what he had asked me and I thought that perhaps he had also asked them the same question. If he had, I am sure they would either have said nothing, or told him that they didn't know. I also didn't know, but I knew what he wanted to hear, and what I must say. I replied;

"Of course you will!. . . Why are you asking me?. . . Surely as Pastor you must know better than I?" . . . I have no doubt you will see your wife again!"

I could sense the almost immediate change in his mood, his tenseness gone and the changed mood in the room. He was smiling, instantly accepting my reply as simple fact, the plain truth. I also knew that I really had no choice in what I had said or done. He hugged me in gratitude and thanked me repeatedly; other eyes in the room were smiling too, but already I felt like a fraud and a liar, a necessary liar! Walking back to my wife's family house, in almost tropical total darkness, reflecting on the minuscule drama I had just witnessed and shared with complete strangers, I was trying to convince myself that I would be forgiven for my dishonesty!

On a recent visit to Rome I visited Diocletian's Baths, now part of the National Roman Museum, and came across a highly detailed exhibition of the development of Mithraism; with the largest collection of religious objects relating to this so-called mystery religion; including sculptures, ritual artefacts and other cultic objects, and of course many illustrative anecdotes. The size of the exhibition was sufficient to keep me occupied for more than half the day, informing me of the extent of devotion to the cult of Mithra, mainly by the ordinary troops of the Roman Army during the first and fourth centuries CE.

Before discovering this exhibition I knew very little about Mithras and Mithraism, but as I followed the arrows of the exhibits, gleaning it's part in the order of things in my mind; almost immediately I sensed a resemblance; a resonance between the rise of the (unofficial) Mithraic Cult running through the legions of the first-century Roman army, and the First World War Tommies, in the trenches on the Somme, with their home-spun spiritual and magical beliefs and Lucky Charms, waiting to go over the top. Both armies using 'unofficial' means of connecting with the numinous and the sacred; as well as accessing talismanic protection against their enemies on the battlefield.

Besides this connection between ordinary soldiers of both armies, two centuries apart, I discovered that both Mithraism and the early Christian Church were feared by the Roman authorities as a threat to the stability of the Roman State; consequently both 'cults' were forced 'underground' as well as both cults competing with each other for general recognition, and acceptance among all the other Roman pagan beliefs, and possibly influencing each other; with Christianity eventually becoming the State Religion, by a hair's breadth!

It is impossible to know how this actually happened historically, but I can imagine the behind-the-scenes discussions, and dealings which might have influenced the Emperor Constantine to become Christian rather than a Mithraist. But had he opted for the 'Persian' rather than the 'Jewish' cult (as they both were at that stage of their development) the historical consequences of a change in his decision would have had direst consequences for the whole of world history. As Michael Caine would say; "Not a lot of people know that!". And there is no good reason why church congregations would need to know this, either or about the Council of Nicea in AD325, as they recite the Nicean Creed, or about the Queen being the Head of the C of E, or of the many small anecdotes that tell the Jesus story, and how or why that story, simply told underwrites two thousand years of European material culture; it's Cities and great buildings, sculptures, paintings, music, poetry, and everything else that together allows us to make sense of our human existence.

Although we might no longer attend church services, as well as we might no longer read sacred literature, but our Christian cultural heritage swims around us, without referencing anything biblical. Such is the density of our Christian culture, whether we know it or like it or otherwise, but if we no longer feel comfortable inside our institutionalised religious buildings, where else can we sustain ourselves through participating in shared communal expressions of the numinous?

I raise this question, not as a matter of intellectual curiosity, but as a genuine existential question, living as I do in a Pre-Reformation (Filipino) Catholic family, surrounded by several (antique) shrines and images, with bookshelves stacked with current historical, sociological, psychological, and religious-studies books and published academic papers, on the post-modern equivalent of squaring the circle; in other words, paying homage to "All things Visible and Invisible", or trying to make sense of Religion after Religion!

My own focus in this has shifted from trying to understand the difference between being 'saved' or 'damned', or in less emotive and more prescient terms; what it is that church-going people believe they are doing when 'worshipping' God, (my own personal difficulties in this is mainly in the language used) or put another way, what are the negative emotional and psychological effects of Modernism's Materialism? These questions, and many others like them have been the bane of my life, and not yet fully addressed, despite having seen the *writing on the wall,* that things cannot continue as they are; just turning up at an empty local parish church and going through the monotonous motions; failing to connect with anything!

I recall reading Peter Berger's book on this difficulty; 'A Rumour of Angels: Modern Society and the Rediscovery of the Supernatural.'(1969), and thinking at the time, that for *Modern* people, who will not be able to pick-up any *'signals of transcendence'* unless they have first acquainted themselves with at least some of the basic ideas of modern religious studies; such as Rudolf Otto's *Idea of the Holy*, or experiences of the *Sacred and the Numinous*. For these are the very basic means of sensitising one's own soul, of making it responsive to any of the many signals of transcendence, which otherwise would remain invisible to us. I am now thinking of E.M.Forster's idea of his epigraphic "Only Connect", as something we should learn from being with others. And once this happens in the way I'm suggesting, it could be experienced as a surprising discovery, as something new, that in the *twinkling of an eye* changes our sense of ourselves and our perceptions of how we see the world. Although these things are invisible to our waking eyes, this hidden side of the world can be seen only through the *eyes of the soul* or the imagination. This is how I see a *modern or postmodern* belief in God, who it seems, for His and our convenience can sometimes appear as not-God, or in some other symbolic form, as expressed negatively by Paul Klee in a short poem.

> "I am an unsymbolic thing.
> My meaning is what I am,
> You turn the magic ring in vain,
> I have no sense!

Klee's main point here is that we cannot simply replace metaphorical Biblical language with symbols, because symbols by themselves signify nothing and communicate nothing, but are necessary because symbols like anecdotes have the capacity for making the invisible *visible* (or the other way round for us) which otherwise would be beyond expression, But if we wish to go beyond that basic, and purely *personal connection* to the divine, then we return to the traditional bigger picture of the old cataclysmic struggle between good and evil, which is at the centres of all major narratives, and consequently their rituals, plus their many shades from; multi-coloured to stark black and white! Best to take one simple idea at a time, such as the Parable of the Ten Virgins, and like Philipp Nicholi, to mull it over, to make of it what we will, and maybe to pen a few lines, or better still write a cantata so that future generations might also be tempted to unravel the mystery!

Philipp Nicholi wrote in his preface, dated 10 August 1598:

"Day by day I wrote out my meditations, found myself, thank God, wonderfully well, comforted in heart, joyful in spirit, and truly content; gave to my manuscript the name and title of a Mirror of Joy... to leave behind me (if God should call me from this world) as a token of my peaceful, joyful, Christian departure, or (if God should spare me in health) to comfort other sufferers whom He should also visit with the pestilence."

The Mirror of Joy.

"Wake, O wake! With tidings thrilling, the watchmen all the air are filling. Arise, Jerusalem arise! Midnight strikes! No more delaying, the hour has come, we hear them saying. Where are ye all, ye virgins wise? The Bridegroom comes in sight. Raise high your torches bright! Alleluya! The Wedding Song swells loud and strong, go forth and join the festal throng."

Nicholi wrote this under the dark shadow of the *Reformation*, but worse was to come in the form of the so-called *Enlightenment,* with its very *visible* erosion of an every day, taken-for-granted awareness of the *invisible;* and the more recent era of *Modernism*, with the loss of (traditional) sacred values. When I attempt to explain to anyone at any time, how and why the social and political processes of secularisation occurred, I try to impress upon them the importance of these three historical signposts (key points in time) of; Reformation, Enlightenment and Modernism. Each of these three were not single definable events, but stages in changed ways of thinking, (ontologies and paradigms) which Max Weber, a German Sociologist, labelled 'Disenchantment of the World'; conveniently described since, as shifts towards increasingly rational ways of *thinking and explaining*; in a word - Secularisation! The social, economic and political consequences of this shift at each stage, wrought cataclysmic changes in how individuals understood themselves and their worlds, especially their religious beliefs and understanding.

Philipp Nicholi's religious understanding was unambiguously certain with no room for doubt, in fact to be doubter in his times was a too dangerous thing; but for us 'Moderns' or 'Post-Moderns', religious faith like social class, is a relative thing, open to considerable doubt. Yet for Nicholi's next generation, another German thinker, Gottfried Wilhelm Leibniz (1646-1716) opened further the debate of religious certainties with his treatise, 'Theodicy: Essays on the Goodness of God, the Freedom of Man and the Origin of Evil' (1710), in which he attempted to reconcile his claim that God, who was an absolutely perfect being, created the best of all possible worlds, and yet also allowed the presence of evil! Briefly put, his argument rested on three basic premises: (1) God is good and benevolent; (2) God is omnipotent and (3) evil is real. Which means that if evil exists, a benevolent God would not want evil to occur, and being omnipotent, He could prevent evil from happening. This gave rise to a perpetual and ongoing debate which is still far from being concluded, which from time to time is melted down and recast anew, to the confusion of both believers and atheists alike. Something along similar lines was also taken up by David Hume (1711-1776), the favourite philosopher of the Scottish Enlightenment, which raised and carried the debate about the 'reasonableness of religious beliefs' to the centre of English philosophy in those times; philosophers including Hutcheson, Hobbes, Mandeville, Locke; whose disputes are now regarded as part of that historical shift towards *positivism* and *scientism*; and ultimately to Nietzsche's philosophy which claimed the 'Death of God', and Charles Darwin's Evolutionism. Since then there has been a gradual restructuring in institutional religious affiliation and practices, as an attempt to remain relevant to daily life of the people, via; the ordination of women, parish churches as soup kitchens, etc. But its all too late! The accumulative damage wrought by the historical combination of reformation, enlightenment and modernism, found all the Christian Churches wanting! All of them, like foolish virgins, unprepared for the Cultural march of European history; that in a nutshell was their undoing. There can be no going back, hoping for a resurrection of their 'nostalgic past' by attempting to serve new wine in old wine-skins!

But that doesn't mean questions about the *invisible* (in a religious context) have gone away; far from it! At some time in the near future it will simply, like God, metamorphose into another Reality. Continuing to taunt and tantalise us, enticing us to pursue it, because it still (surprisingly) just about exists; perhaps hidden or sleeping! For a start it wont be called religion, and God wont be referred to as God; its most likely form more like a poetical abstraction, more a feeling than a concept or idea. It will float in the wind like hints of half remembered scents, entering their sensibility like whispering pentecostal murmurs. Future generations might not recognise them for what they are; *reverberations of a redundant god or gods.* They might think it is something they have eaten or been bitten by, unless of course they themselves are a particular kind of poet, or composer of music, or painter or designer, of whatever has come to replace the traditional arts.They will assume it might be a redundant remnant of modern or post-modern consciousness; or a product of their redundant Brave New World in which they themselves have become some kind of little gods!

Their language will be cool but its message will be disturbingly uncool, more like something from the far distant past, something invisibly beyond the power of their ultra- modern technology or understanding to delete. Perhaps something closer to their superior digitalised robotic language which will be totally flummoxed by a persistence of the redundant *notion of soul,* as an entity beyond explanation of binary grammars. Consequently the only modern way to deal with the 'impossibly difficult' notion of 'soul' as word and concept, would be to delete it completely from all future vocabularies. Even if in some way it would render the last two thousand years of western human creativity meaningless; reducing the remaining differences between our Homo Sapiens species and our forthcoming companions and masters; the so-call Humanoid Robots! At least this will complete the current Cycle of the Death of God and the subsequent Death of Institutional Religion. All is change! That is the basic message that underwrites the sacred and the numinous in our post Christian era; simple to declare but difficult to comprehend and to realise. Philosophically it is the half way point between Being and Non- Being, or in modern Binary terms, mid point between Zero and One. The point at which conventional 'meanings' in everyday language breaks free of its corrupted moorings, to re-instate and refine the mythopoetic language of the tribe.

To review the current status of the dialectic of the *Visible and the Invisible*, it is perhaps safer for me to consider this in simple terms that I understand; my question is; are they now redundant? That mystical dichotomy, now condemned to the dusty language of the Nicene Creed of the English Book of Prayer, hurriedly uttered or muttered in church services up and down the country, disconnected from thought or emotion, spoken and soon forgotten! Apart from the obvious spiritual consequences of this, there is the moral and cultural decline in social mores associated with modern changing values implicit in ordinary language, even at its simplest levels of social relationships, in how we treat one another in public spaces. In my own town-centre (Reading) it is normal for pedestrians to be treated as *objects* in the bustling pedestrian streets, paradoxically reversing my kind of reality, that is from my visible self, to something less-so; as a virtually *invisible* anonymous body- obstacle, to be manoeuvred-around to make way for others.

In those two words, the *visible* and *invisible* juxtaposed; simply those two plain words alone, there is the sacred code for the continuity of human existence; from one generation to the next, the circle of life if you will? *That code spans time and life from the beginning of the world till eternity,* when perhaps we shall all become invisible, but in the meantime, present and future generations might seek. It all depends on them being prepared for the darkness, and having sufficient oil for their lamps.

On a lighter note, and before the lights are completely extinguished, there is still plenty that illuminates everyday life; that is if the 'frenetic pedestrians' in my town-centre are capable of sparing one tiny moment from their relentlessly busy daily schedule, for a little psychological, emotional, or even spiritual refreshment, in the form of *reflective thinking* that might begin with the simple act of reading or listening to a poem. Will it work, I imagine the 'frenetic pedestrians' demanding to know! The obvious response is, "Suck it and see!" If they can manage the time of day! They might even ask, "How or why might it work?" The answer again is simple! It works because poetry is fundamentally *the premier carrier of consciousness;* when we read or listen to a poem, the combination of word-rhythms and word-images influence the flow of our thoughts and body rhythms; affecting even our pulse rate, and if we continue reading, thinking about it's meaning, at some point it begins to change how we think about ourselves and how we relate to one another. A line of poetry becomes a kind of mantra that sustains us through times of doubt and sorrow!

Following the period (1715-1789) we now refer to as the 'Enlightenment' and the 'Age of Reason', beginning with Newtons's "Principia Mathematica', and the 'writings' of the French Philosophes, especially Voltaire (who ironically also liked writing poetry), which sparked the French and American Revolutions, and panicked the rest of the Kingdoms of Europe, including Britain; there was, besides the obvious *visible* social and political reactions, an almost *invisible* poetic response to the deeper spiritual and psychological climate of the English Nation; for example as caught in the poetry of Coleridge, Wordsworth, and Blake.

I have enjoyed my retirement from teaching for quite a few years now. Its greatest benefit is not having to hurry my 'preparations for the day.' This privileged status permits me to lie in bed in the morning for as long as I wish, but as I continue to wake-up as soon as it begins to get light outside, and the birds begin their morning chorus, I usually have at least an hour for shifting gently in and out of sleep; a state known as Hypnogogia, in other words on the threshold of consciousness. For me, this includes, daydreaming, lucid thinking, philosophising, reverie, meditating, mulling-over, pondering, poetising, and much else that allows me access to two worlds, or states of consciousness; the Visible and the Invisible, or the Seen and the Hidden!

During these moments when my consciousness seems to expand and my mind takes in the world with a rare and strange intensity, anything might happen in my mind! The French poet Baudelaire describe this experience as 'privileged moments' in his essay 'The Poem of Hashish'. "There are days when we wake up with 'a young and vigorous genius. We have hardly opened our eyes when we are impressed by the strong relief, precise outlines and rich coloured in the world around us. The moral world too seems full of new illuminations. Compared to the 'heavy shadows of common everyday existence', such states can justly be called paradisiac. They are rare and fleeting, and their most curious feature is that they occur without any visible or definable cause.' But in my case they come only during sunrise, in the half-light of dawn; I see in the dark like a cat!

The French poet/philosopher Paul Valery called these moments 'the purest states of the Self', regarding them as 'basic to the poet's experience, *as if we fall out of this world and into another*. In privileged moments, everything suddenly ceases to have its usual effect, their meanings change, colours change, and personal relationships change; sounds have a musical timbre, colours speak, and perfumes hint of strange ideas. Other poets also refer to their experiences of musical harmony; for me, my epiphanies are mostly expressed through words of songs, as if the musicality of experiences are grounded in the background music of remembered actual events! As Baudelaire observed, "Music gives the idea of space." In this, there is more than a hint of that something of the experiences of religious mystics; for example of Phillip Nicholi, or even the transitory exaltation experienced by a young schoolboy's hymn-singing during cold morning school-hall assemblies. Or as described in detail in Flaubert's first 'Temptation of St Anthony'. "The object you were contemplating seemed to encroach on yours, you bent closer to it, and links formed; you clasped one another, touching each other by innumerable delicate adherences; then, through looking so intently, you no longer saw anything; listening, you heard nothing, and your mind itself finally lost notion of particularity which kept it alert. It was like an immense harmony engulfing you soul with marvellous palpitations, and you felt in its plenitude an inexpressible comprehension of the unrevealed wholeness of things; the interval between you and the object, like an abyss closing, grew narrower and narrower, until the difference vanished, because you both were bathed in infinity; you penetrated each other equally, and a subtle current passed from you into matter while the life of the elements slowly pervaded you, rising like a sap; one degree more, and you would have become nature, or nature become you."

'St Anthony's Temptation' might also be seen in more general terms, as moments of ecstasy in our own personal reveries and other dream experiences; our common or uncommon experiences, as seen through a poet's eye. It refreshes our imagination, because for a moment we transcend the limits of our ordinary daily discourse. Or as Gaston Bachelard, in his 'The Poetics of Space' suggests;

"An unexpected literary image can so move the spirit that it will follow the induction of tranquility. In fact the literary image can make the spirit sufficiently sensitive to receive unbelievably fine impressions. Thus, in a remarkable passage, Gabriele D'Annunzio, (World War One Soldier Poet: — The Poet; or Il Profeta, [The Prophet] makes us see the look in the eyes of a trembling hare which, in a torment-free instant, projects peace over the entire autumnal world.

He writes: 'Did you ever see a hare in the morning, leave the freshly ploughed furrows, run a few seconds over the silvery frost, then stop in silence, sit down on its hind legs, prick up its ears and look at the horizon? Its gaze seems to confer Peace upon the entire universe! And it would be hard to think of a surer sign of deep peace than this motionless hare which, having declared a truce with its eternal disquiet, sits observing the steaming countryside. At this moment, it is a *sacred animal*, one that should be worshipped.'.' The dreamer who lets his musing follow this line of vision will experience an immensity of outspread fields in a higher key!

Remarkably, such was the same scene one very early cold damp Tuesday morning, 18th September 1956, when I was young and eager Royal Navy Airman, taxiing my Sky-raider aircraft along the Perimeter Track surrounding Culdrose Naval Air Station, towards the main runway, making ready for take-off, in preparation to joining HMS Albion,(awaiting four Skyraider aircraft of 849 squadron, C Flight), somewhere in the Atlantic Ocean, in preparation for what would eventually be called, Operation Musketeer, the Battle for the Suez Canal.

The only thing I remember of that morning were the dozens hares sitting in the frozen long grass on the perimeter of the airfield. At that time of the early morning the airfield was as usual, covered by a heavy blanket of damp-fog-like grey mist, native to Cornwall's Lands-End, The Lizard. The ground glistening with hoarfrost, all illuminated by a wan yellow dawn-sunlight breaking through the mist; creating a kind of eerie pale-yellow halo. It was in this arena of eerie grey mist, that the only movements of natural life were the hares bobbing about. On hearing our aircraft trundling along their frozen turf, unusual for them at that time of the early morning, they suddenly became still. Sitting upright on their haunches, motionless, perhaps to their minds invisible! But I could see clearly their dew-soaked scraggy damp fur, their wide-eyed observant gaze, their frozen contemplation, their ears pricked. This was D'Annuncio's vision!

In a letter to Clara Rilke, Rilke wrote: "Works of art always spring from those who have faced the danger, gone to the very end of an experience, to the point beyond which no human being can go. The further one dares go, the more decent, the more personal, the more unique a life becomes." An ability to see things from the outside and the inside!

Merleou-Ponty the phenomenological thinker, hints in his final meandering thoughts shortly before he died, how this might develop; outlined in his sketch titled, 'The Visible and the Invisible', and before then his explanation for the Chiasm, the Crossover; where for example, one mode of something crosses over another, in the way that a nerve crosses over a vein in the human body; as he remarks; 'never making it quite clear when the metaphorical passes over to the actual and physical'. It is through this Janus-like ability for seeing things from within and without, that is at the heart of phenomenology and at the centre of human consciousness, and which draws on the 'imaginary' for our understanding of human agency and events; with it's accompanying enigma that some people are just naturally better, or luckier at this than others! They will perhaps inform you that it is either insight or intuition, or a sixth-sense; or perhaps merely their circumstantial and existential attempt of staying in touch.

My most singular powerful personal experience of this sort was during my Military Service time in the flying branch of the Royal Navy, just after Suez, whilst flying American Skyraiders, (AEW's) aircraft from H.M.S. Albion, in the Artic Sea, just inside the Artic Circle; by today's standards, the antique-looking propeller-driven Skyraider, launched from a Light-Fleet Centaur-Class Carrier might be considered amateur stuff; but for me, in those weather and sea conditions being there was considerably more scary!

H.M.S. Albion (also by modern standards, a relatively small aircraft carrier,) had been battened - down for nearly the entire week, in other words the heavy seas and extreme weather conditions making flying-stations impossible for several days. During that time there had been no let-up in the weather, and yet the ship kept cruising resolutely further north into increasingly severely bad weather. Yet for some inexplicable reason someone at some point somewhere onboard decided, at that indefinable point we would recommence Flying-Stations, despite the heavy pitching, rolling and yawing of the ship and the howling gale gusting across the Flight-Deck night and day, with a build-up of thick ice on the several aircraft tethered with triple lashings to the Flight-Deck. Working conditions were such that it was near impossible to walk, or even stand-up unsupported when the ship was ploughing directly into wind, with more than forty knots of a freezing-cold gale gusting across the Deck.

Thankfully Skyraiders are very heavy American aircraft, built like army tanks, with massive flaps, and consequently remarkably manoeuvrable when in the air, with solid stability, even in the harshest flying conditions. My aircraft was first on the catapult for launching that morning; port-side Number One steam-catapult, requiring considerable preparation manoeuvring and man-handling of the aircraft to make ready for the launch, everthing taking much longer than usual in attaching the metal sling to the undercarriage, connecting the aircraft to the catapult. Besides this difficulty, the unremitting roll and yaw of the ship making it difficult to 'time' the exact moment for operating the catapult, driving the aircraft forward to correspond with the ship's rising-bow to its zenith, thus sending the aircraft on an upward flight-path. (Obviously if the timing is out of phase, the aircraft will be sent on a downward trajectory). This 'phasing' wasn't so critical for Skyraiders as for the Jets, (which were lighter aircraft), because the Skyraider, with it's massive flaps producing maximum lift as soon as it reaches flight speed, thrusting it into the air even before reaching the end of its travel on the catapult.

The dancing, bucking, rocking movement of the ship and the heavy side-wind across the flight deck added to difficulties in moving aircraft around positioning them on the catapult. The Flight Deck Officer, who controls the launching and recovery of aircraft, was at this time being held upright by two very sturdy aircraft 'Handlers', (whose main task is to physically move aircraft around the Deck). The FDO was battling against the wind and sea-spray as he flagged me into the launch- position. He signalled Brakes-On, circled his hand for me to fully open the engine throttle for launching. I was ready to go, and felt the catapult take up it's slack. With engine at full Boost and flaps fully down; I could feel my aircraft shaking violently as if caught in a heaving vortex, by each wave crashing over the bow of the ship and reducing visibility in the bow-mist. I could just about make-out the outline of the bow rising against the dark sea, its gigantic raging sea-sprays almost obliterating the skyline. Intermittently I was virtually blinded by the barrage of mist soaking my cockpit canopy and windscreen; unable to see the Flight Deck Officer or anything else. Eventually I was ready for 'Go', I glimpsed the Flight Deck Officer's flag thrust downwards through the sea-mist; bracing myself, holding the control column stiffly between my knees in a neutral position, I was off. In less than a minute on the catapult, I was airborne and climbing clear of the bow of the ship, and veering slightly to port. Apart from the salt-spray on my windscreen, once airborne I was at least free from the wind and sea conditions buffeting the ship. I could already feel the intense coldness in my legs; my screen rapidly icing-up. I immediately reported this to Flight Control, and they instructed to circuit whilst the rest of the launch continued, in preparation for possible cancellation of my sortie.

The landing circuit is basically four left turns, bringing the aircraft back to a flight-path parallel with the ship; and onto the final leg, bringing me back on a parallel course, slightly starboard of the ship; altitude around 5000 feet from which I could view the launch of a Sea Venom, at the exact moment when separating from the catapult; it looked ridiculously small compared to the other Skyraiders of my squadron awaiting launching in Fly One, on the starboard side of the Deck, forward of the Island.

The Venom had an unusual arrangement for its aircrew, the pilot's cockpit offset on the lefthand side of the fuselage and a flush door for the Observer, with a single jet engine set in mid-fuselage behind the cockpits, and air intakes in the mainplane roots either side of the fuselage, which if hit by sufficient sea-spray, would soak the engine causing an immediate 'flameout' in the engine. I had often thought about the possibility of this when observing Sea Venom launches, which unfortunately now, at the very moment I was observing its vulnerability, what I had so-many times feared, was actually happening!

From my position above the Carrier, a sole Skyraider flying at less than a thousand feet above and alongside the ship and peering-down, my unique view of the ship; better than anyone else on the Flight Deck, I saw the giant bow-waves breaking over the forecastle, (front of the Flight Deck) with each downward movement of the ship's bow, a massive wall of sea-spray with each dipping heave of the bow already soaking the minute Venom whilst waiting on the catapult, As I drew-up, abreast of the bow, the ship suddenly shuddered and dropped deeply into a recoiling wave; my last glimpse of the aircraft was of it slicing the waves, as it ploughed into the sea on a downward path, having left the catapult on the sudden dropping of the bow.There must have been an immediate flameout; the Sea-Venom instantly swallowed-up by the dark grey waves, condemning the crew to an immediate death in the frozen depths of the Artic Ocean.

No other eyes had witnessed the whole scene. The attitude of the flight-deck, the turgid movement of the catapult, the aircraft on its shallow dipping path of flight, and its sudden rapid disappearance! I shuddered as I watched it sink! The ship rapidly, but pointlessly altered course to starboard; the rescue helicopter also impossibly scanning the seething wash from the rapid turning of the ship. Within minutes, it was all too obvious that they were already on the bottom of the frozen ocean, already deep-frozen, preserved for eternity. But I could still see them in my mind's eye, for I myself merely minutes before, had been catapulted, not downward, but fortunately up into the air from that very catapult, in almost identical conditions, now imagining myself sharing their same fate!

My next problem was returning to the ship! I had already seen the state of the Landing Mirror, and realised that I wouldn't be able to maintain a sufficiently clear view for a normal recovery; and that if I were to attempt a Deck-Landing in those sea-conditions that it would be dangerously risky! There was no other choice, because I knew I was out of range of other possible landing strips; the only alternative would be being 'Talked-Down' by the Flight-Deck Officer, (FDO), who I knew to be a very experienced Navy pilot. He now came on the RT and explained the conditions for Recovery. As we spoke I could see that the Aircraft-Handlers were rigging an emergency Barricade, a Safety Net, made of metal cables with tough webbing straps which formed a kind of flexible net capable of 'catching' an aircraft in an emergency; and this certainly was an emergency!

I completed my landing circuit and was on the correct glide-slope, as far as I could see, which if I maintained it, should take me to the correct point of contact for catching one of the arrestor-wires The ship had reduced speed somewhat, and this to some extent steadied her, although she was still bucking and rocking; rising-up on a series of waves, and then dropping suddenly, as if the angry sea's-energy had suddenly dissipated; the ship falling back into its trough, like a massive dead whale being thrown back into the deep.This sometimes happens even in less heavy seas, but obviously more a problem when accompanied by sudden heavy gusting sidewinds, and low-visibility. I had already thought my way through this scenario several times, whilst I had been observing the loss of the Venom; trying to talking myself out of 'shitting myself" with fear! The Flight Deck Officer's voice came over the RT, instructing me he would 'Talk' me down, keeping me informed how I looked from his location in front of the frozen Landing Mirror, which in those conditions was now redundant. He could see how sudden gusting side-winds shifted me off the glide-scope; and could see deviations from central line of flight relative to the Flight Deck, bringing me back on line, with a'left or right bits of shouted instructions!

Finally I was within five hundred feet or so of the landing spot, and on more or less on what seemed to be the correct Glidescope. I was keeping my focus through the sea spray on the space, midway between the first and second arrester wires and the Safety Barrier; but the ship was bucking as if she was writhing from an injury; I could see the Deck rising to meet me. If I was lucky I might catch a wire just before the ship hit another trough. One final small adjustment on the control column, then the 'pull' of the arrestor wire. Luckily I was back-down, followed by a bone-shaking thud as my main wheels hit the Deck; I was safe, throttling back, and alive, thank God!

For how many flights and nights immediately afterwards did I see them, preserved in the frozen deep, strapped frozen in their cockpits of their sunken Sea Venom. Imagining myself a Merman drifting in the deep, or sometimes as Dylan Thomas's 'Captain Cat, at 'his window thrown wide to the sun and the disappeared seas he had sailed long ago, when his eyes, like mine, were blue with bright slumberland voyages; ear-ringed and rolling in every naughty port and twines, sounds with the drowned and blowsy-breasted dead. Poor Captain Cat, with me also weeping and sleeping as we sail, amid Sea Shanties from the Last Night of the Proms, or like Drake in his hammock seeing it all so plainly as he saw it long ago!' 'But Jesus was a sailor! When he walked upon the water / and he spent a long time watching from his lonely wooden tower. And when he knew for certain only drowning men could see him, he said; All men will be sailors then until the sea shall free them / but he himself was broken long before the sky would open / forsaken, almost human, he sank beneath our wisdom like a stone, in the frozen arctic seas!

I mention this tragic incident of my one-time difficult Deck Landing, only to make a point, (impossible otherwise to make!) that phenomenological thinking is necessarily a consequence of an actual *experience*, a real life experience of 'presence', of being there; nicely summed-up for our deliberations in Martin Heidegger's term - Dasein, (being there); with no remotely comparative, later experience in academia or any other job, which would allow me to make such a poetical point!

But is it necessary to go and look for 'danger' other than the danger of writing, of expressing oneself? *Doesn't the poet put language in danger?* Doesn't he utter words that are dangerous? Hasn't the fact that, for so long, poetry's been the echo of heartache, given it a pure dramatic tonality? When it is possible to really live in a poetic image, we learn to know, in each of its tiny fibres, a becoming of Being, that is an awareness of the Being's inner disturbance. Here Being is so sensitive that it is upset by a word. In the same letter, Rilke adds: "This sort of *derangement,* (disturbance) which is peculiar to us humans, it must go into our work." Reading a poem is only a first stage of recovery from despair; afterwards comes 'Reflective thinking'; not unlike peering into a metaphorical mirror or deep pool of still water; asking our reflection how does it feel. How does it feel? Poetry sustains us in this difficult task; it has a mysterious way of entering the invisible bloodstream of the soul, if you will permit such an oxymoron? I should add that I disagree with Freud when he claims that dreams are the royal road to the unconscious, as the location of our deepest fears and hopes. Instead I would choose Poetry as *the most direct route*; for the poetic mode speaks to our whole Being; body, mind and soul, via the unconscious mind; the receptacle for our mixed memories. But we don't even have to delve that deep, it is simpler and more straight forward than that; enough to know that through the plain and simple act of reading a poem, something happens to how we feel about ourselves, and how we connect or relate to others. Of course it is mysterious, and most probably we wonder why and how? For a brief moment in time, we transcend our mundane circumstances, sharing the poet's glimpse 'of a world in a grain of sand and heaven in a flower, to hold infinity in the palm of your hand, and eternity in an hour.'

William Blake wrote those words! He also wrote the words to the hymn Milton, known as 'Jerusalem'; played at the close of the 'Last Night of The Proms' every year, a hymn for everyone; he would be so pleased if he knew that! He was a man of the people; an engraver of printing plates, an artist, a mystical poet. As a free thinker, almost the singular prophetic voice opposed to the 'Iron Cage' of early capitalism, at that time wreaking havoc in the lives of the common people. He was also devoutly religious in singularly independent way, challenging the national Church, the Church of England, by reinterpreting the Gospels as social anecdotes for daily living. His independence grew out of his working-class family background, and growing up and living in a renown (rough)' tradesmen's district of London, where for most of his life, he was surrounded by an anti-hegemonic social and political environment, of (sometimes) exotic Radical Dissenting circles, consisting of; Quakers, Muggletonians, Millenaries, Sabbatarians or Seventh-Day Men, Thraskites, Adams's (whose meeting-place was'Paradise' and whose devotions were made in nakedness), Seekers, Ranters (who condemned the Bible and called it ironically 'The Divine Legacy') Brownists, Tryonists (vegetarians), the 'Circle of the First-Born' (Behemists), Salmonists, 'Heavenly-Father-Men' (whose whole emphasis was on Mercy) and 'Children of the New Birth', most given to meditation and 'Visions of Angels and Representations'. And other 'Sweet Singers of Israel'- very poetically given to turning all into Rhyme, and singing all their Worship. (They met in an Ale-House and eat, and drink and smoke.) This rich mixture of anti-establishment Christians re-shaped Blake's Biblical ideas into producing his own poetical-mystical understanding and his way of life, "Without Ceremonies at all" The social historian E.P.Thompson suggests, that with these influences, it is understandable that Blake produced his peculiar vocabulary of symbolism, and that his strongest influence, the Bible - but the Bible read in a particular way; as influenced by Milton and radical Dissent which included; Moravians, Baptists, Philadelphians and Behemists, and hence to Swedenborgians. Besides these influences, Blake himself was widely read, including; Neo-Platonists, Kabbalistic and Hermetic sources, all within the Neoplatonists tradition. It was also within this exotic literary alchemy that he sensed, perhaps from Milton, an analogy between the English and Jews, each in their own way seen as the 'Chosen People of God'; Blake replacing Israel with England. Also his Druidical studies that led him to the idea that England was the original Zion, the Holy Land. He wrote; "All things Begin and End in Albion's Ancient Druid Rocky Shore". 'The fields from Islington Marybone, |To Primrose Hill and Saint John's Wood. |Were builded over with pillars of gold. |And there Jerusalem pillars stood, Here Little-ones ran on the fields. The Lamb of God among them seen.| And fair Jerusalem his Bride:| Among the meadows green.

Willian Blake (1757 - 1827), was contemporaneous with Samuel Taylor Coleridge (1772 - 1834), of Jesus College Cambridge, and William Wordsworth (1770 - 1850) of St. Johns College, Cambridge, (also Poet Laureate); but although by their definition Blake would be considered unschooled, and probably uncouth, he outshone them in depth and numinosity of his thoughts, words, and images. As Leo Damrosch comments in his book, Eternity's Sunrise - The Imaginative World of William Blake (2015), "Blake condenses an important part of his message into four eloquent lines:;

> He who binds to himself a joy
> Does the wing'ed life destroy,
> But he who kisses the joy as it flies
> Lives in Eternity's sunrise.

In his book, "Eternity's Sunrise", Damrosch comments:

"Blake believed that we lived in the midst of Eternity right now and that if we could open our consciousness to the fulness of being, it would be like experiencing a sunrise that never ends. That would not be a mystical escape *from* reality — he was never mystical in that sense —but a fuller and deeper engagement with *reality*. Yet he also knew how hard it is to relinquish the self - centred possessiveness that kills joy instead of kissing it, and much of his work focuses on that struggle."

Both Wordsworth and Coleridge, also claimed to be reactionaries against the repressive society of early capitalism, each of them lightly touching on a spiritual dimension, who also must have read some of Blake's poetry, were by comparison 'limpid' souls. Wordsworth began his 'Intimations' with; "Our birth is but a sleep and a forgetting"; his stated religious beliefs 'inspiring' him to categorically announce; "I am willing to shed my blood for the established Church of England!", and commenting on Blake on hearing that he had died;

"There was no doubt that this poor man was mad, but there is something in the madness that interests me more than the saints of Lord Byron and Walter Scott," As for Coleridge, who apparently had been loaned a copy of Blake's "Songs of Innocence and of Experience", and who briefly met Blake on one occasion, was insufficiently moved to offer any remarks on Blake's poetry whatsoever!

The nearest poet to Blake of his era, perhaps is Gerald Manley Hopkins, (1844 - 1889) but he, still far-far away from Blake. Hopkins was also 'mystical' within the tradition of Catholic thinkers; he was first and foremost a Jesuit Priest, a closet-Poet perhaps? He grew up in Stratford Essex, studied Classics at Balliol College Oxford, converted from Anglican to Roman Catholic, and suffered throughout his short life as a priest with problems of religious doubt; his poetry that of a Soul in Free fall, and without a parachute! Not seeing the world in a grain of sand, but "Nature as a Heraclitean Fire and of Comfort of the Resurrection — Cloud-puffball, torn tufts pillows | flaunt forth, then chevy on an air built thoroughfare, heaven-roisterers, in gay -gangs | they through; they glitter inmates down dazzling white wash, wherever an elm arches, shiverlights and shadow tackle in long|lashes lace, and pair." His unbearable anguish and emotional pain self evident in every line he wrote, constantly recycling elements of a deeply felt liturgy and the forthcoming blazing fire!

Whenever I read any works of mystical poets I immediately look for a religious tap-root! As Northrop Frye, the Canadian literary theorist and critic points out;

"In poetry the word is a complex of ideas and images, ambiguous and associative in meaning, synthetically apprehended." Supposedly self-evident in modern times, when poems and songs are represented through the modern idioms of; Cinema, Theatre, Musicals, Pop-concerts and other modern mass media. Especially 'Musicals' which contain implicitly (if not explicitly) religious lyrics and stirring melodies, performed using powerful dramatic moments, such as in 'Joseph and the Amazing Technicolour Dreamcoat', (1968), 'Jesus Christ Superstar', (1970), 'Evita', (1976), 'Les Miserables,' which has run for 34 years in London's West End Theatres; each of it's songs, with haunting sentiments becoming emotional icons; recalled and sung by almost everyone everywhere, even if they've never read Victor Hugo's original novel, or seen the show. But the poetry of the powerful lyrics and emotionally tragic stories are now lodged deeply in the nation's consciousness; so much so that anyone can replay them in their head anytime they feel moved! "From the table in the corner, They could see a world reborn, And they rose with voices ringing, And they can hear them now, . . The very words that they have sung became their last communion on this lonely barricade at dawn. Oh my friends, . .my friends forgive me, That I live and you are gone. There's a Grief that can't be spoken, And there's . . . etc.

But for me, the combination of poetry and music most evidently as *signals of transcendence* is in 'Folk', both old and new, as in powerful ballads, such as those of Bob Dylan (awarded the Nobel Prize for Literature 2016, for '*having created new poetic expressions within the great American song tradition*), and more! Dylan tapped into the rebellious mood of American youth in the 1960s, grew-up in a traditional Jewish household, even celebrating his 'bar mitzvah', and sensing winds of change, sucking-up eclectic anecdotes from all available sources; from his school books- of 'Moby Dick', 'Catcher in The Rye', Iliad and 'Odyssey'; and from Cinema,' The Graduate,' etc., his graphic word-images resonating the power of the *invisible* "Of War and Peace the truth just twists. Its curfew gull it glides. Upon four-legged forest clouds, the cowboy angel rides. With his candle lit into the Sun, Though it's Glow is waxed in black, All except when Neath the trees of Eden." And to "Sara, Sara, Sweet Virgin angel, love of my life. Sara, Sara, Radiant jewel, Mystical wife", or deep down in the gutter of 'Desolation Row', where: "They're selling postcards of the hanging,| painting the passports brown.|The beauty parlour filled with sailors,| the circus is in town. Here comes the blind commissioner, they've got him in a trance. One hand tied to the tight-rope walker, the other in his pants. And the Riot Squad, their restless, . . . they need somewhere to go, as lady and I look out tonight from Desolation Row." (If you know it, hum it!)

Also for theatre-goers, the syllabus of Drama is inclusive; each a dramatic Time-Capsule in which the *invisible,* communicated through spoken words and live actions, on stage, its time-line stretching all the way back to the very earliest roots of our civilisation in it's the earliest attempts to identify the sources of the numinous, through to the most advanced form of communication of the *invisibly sacred,* through the *moving image,* in which the essence of our beliefs in the juxtaposition of the *Visible and the Invisible,* lie deep beneath every *poetical image;* even in the most ordinary anecdote or banal story, like vaporous will-o-the-wisp *puff-balls,* carried by currents of air, either in plain-words and actions, or in their newest forms of Mass Media; such as the hyperreal Dolby-Atmos Sound Cinema films, Video Games, Virtual Reality, and whatever next, in its various forms, all the way through to future synthetic Humanoid Robots with their artificial consciousnesses, their *messages* constructed and stored digitally, resurrected electronically and made visible via complex and expensive wizardry: or otherwise awaiting downloading from some metaphorical Cloud!

But one hopes, there could be a return to the genuinely mystical, through a reappraisal of the existence of 'the soul', not as metaphor but as existential reality; as Henry Corbin's theorising demands; "We must restore to the soul its complete integrity, which is to say that we must definitively allow once again its intrinsic and undeniable *reality,* and that must be the place where the divine appears. From this, the second condition follows logically, which is to restore to *imagination* its status, which is to be a mediator between the World and God, between Creation and Creator. (But take care! It's not just any imagination and certainly not the *imaginary* that we usually designate by this term.) This means moreover that the creature - that is, man in this case - avails himself of an *Active Imagination*, an imagination's agent that fills the space of the soul. By engendering its own world of visions and illumination; the soul rediscovers the too often forgotten angel as divine manifestation. The "interworld" created in this way was sought above all by Henry Corbin — his *imaginal world*, whose name he adopted from high medieval philosophy. It is a world where spirit is incarnated and body is spiritualised, an inter-world (between the visible and the invisible) that we also call, according to tradition, the world of *subtle bodies*.

(Subtle bodies are best characterised as an invisible 'spiritual layer' inherent in physical bodies, best explained as something experienced phenomenologically)

Phenomenology studies structures of conscious experience, as experienced from the first-person point of view. Along with relevant conditions of experience; the central structure of which is its intentionality, that is the way it is directed through its content or meaning toward a certain object in the world.

We all experience various types of *experience*; including perception, imagination, thought, intuition, emotion, desire, volition, and action. Thus, the domain of phenomenology is a range of experiences including these types (among others). Personal experience includes not only relatively passive experience as seen or heard, but also active experience as in walking or hammering a nail, or kicking a ball. (The range will be specific to each species of being that enjoys consciousness; our focus is on our own, human experience. Not all conscious-beings will, or will be able to, practice phenomenology, as we do.) Conscious experiences have a unique feature: _we experience_ them, we live through them or perform them. Other things in the world we may observe and engage, but we do not experience them, in the sense of living through or performing them. This *experiential or first-person feature*—that of being experienced—is an essential part of the nature, or structure of our conscious experience: as we say, "I see / think / desire / do …" This feature is both a phenomenological and an ontological feature of each experience: it is part of what it is for the experience to be experienced (phenomenological) and part of what it is for the experience to be (ontological). And in Theatre or Cinema we see and hear and feel and reflect and share with others who are doing the same thing, enabling us to empathise and connect physically and metaphysically with both the film and other viewers sharing the same viewing-experience with us. In the light of this we can see how modern Cinema has become the supreme medium as the Carrier of Consciousness; transforming one kind of reality into another, that of Images with the power to penetrate the foundations of our unconscious memories, so that events that we did not actually witness become memories that we remember as our own, as if we were actually there! One example of this for me was the 'Dunkirk Evacuation', which happened when I was two years old, but seems to me as if it is part of my own memories of the last war. These somehow, not quite my own memories, were reinvigorated on watching Joe Wright's Film 'Atonement', adapted from Ian McEwan's novel of 2001, the most chilling and penetrating of which was the hypnotic five minute single tracking-shot of the Beach Scene, showing the desolation and desperation of stranded Allied soldiers, every single one of them exhausted and broken, and not knowing their fate, as the German Army closed in on them; trapped and nowhere to go but the sea. Waiting and hoping to be saved but knowing that there were no naval ships available! And then the miracle of the flotilla of hundreds of small boats from British rivers and ports; sailing boats and fishing boats, small motor boats, in fact almost any boat; some from the Thames where I lived! An impossible flotilla of hundreds of these tiny privately owned vessels steaming across the English Channel, each one to carry home a few surviving soldiers.

As the camera sweeps across the beach, pausing for a moment and taking in several incidents; the despairing and worn-out wounded soldiers, their horses being shot, men languishing on the damp sand; a tired and worn-out army hoping for survival, and amidst this chaotic hell the sound of men's voices singing a hymn, a hymn I knew from my own school-day, and almost certainly remembered by the screenwriter Christopher Hampton, who had closed the beach scene with a hovering shot of the Bandstand; also something familiar to a past generation. Men were standing under the canopy of the Bandstand and singing their hearts out, my old school hymn, 'Dear Lord and Father of Mankind.' I knew the hymn from my school morning Assemblies, but I knew nothing about it except that it is Hymn number 383 in the fat green hymn book, 'The English Hymnal.' And then a kind of mental journey began; beginning with Wikipedia which informed me that the words had been taken from a longer poem: *The Brewing of Soma,* by the American Quaker poet John Greenleaf Whittier. With a name like that, and he a Quaker, writing poems about Soma, how could I leave the journey there?

Soma was a sacred ritual drink in Vedic religion, with hallucinogenic properties, and which was drunk by the Vedic priests in their attempt to connect with the divine, and strangely it was this ritual that Whittier referred to in the opening lines of his poem, and which he then compares with the more powerful Christian experience of, "the whisper of Thy call.", and the stirring last verse which reverberates in the closing shot on that Beach.

"Breath through the hearts of our desire Thy coolness and Thy balm. Let sense be numb, let flesh retire; Speak through the earthquake, wind, and fire, O still, small voice of calm! O still, small voice of calm."

My guess is that this either means what it says, or it is meaningless, depending on each of our ontologies; but whatever our religious sensitivities (some or none) it resonates at some deeper affective level. Not because of its religious significance but because the film's music and mood, and the whole mise-en-scene of the film's Beach, with all of its implications and ramifications, which communicated the sheer hopelessness of the event, and when all else seems to have failed, there was always, (for even the least religious of the exhausted soldiers), and for us film-watchers, the haunting tune, "Repton" by Hubert Parry, and the equally haunting words of, 'Dear Lord and Father of Mankind. . .'.

But the journey doesn't quite finish here; for the journey's trail took me yet further on to Holywell Cemetry, next to St. Cross Church in Oxford, where many old Oxfordians are buried; among them Max Muller, Philologist and Orientalist, Fellow at All Soul's College, and Sanskrit Scholar, who translated the sacred Vedas, which returned me to the start of my journey because John Greenleaf Whittier's poem opens with a quote from that very same Rigveda, attributed to Vasishtha:

These libations mixed with milk have been prepared for Indra:
Offers Soma to the drinker of Soma (Rv.vii.trans. Max Muller)

I wonder if the richness of these ancient resonances are in any way responsible for the hairs on my neck standing on end, when imbibing resonances of the closing-shot of the Beach Scene from the film Atonement? It is because filmic scenes such as these, that I am further convinced that the future of a 'Public Religion' will cease to be what we ordinarily understand as 'acts of worship' in those almost redundant old cold-stone buildings, to perhaps become something different, something new, potentially powerfully shared experiences of the *Numinous* in those lush temples we presently call Cinemas. Places where people congregate, to be moved, shaken, and stirred; for modern Cinema has finally become the supreme medium as a carrier of consciousness; with myth the original source of all beliefs, which is how the things we believe-in, might at last become Visible, become (filmic) Flesh!

Cinemas now show more than films, they show live theatre, opera and dance, by relaying shows in real-time, as if viewed from a Front Seat. In the cinema advertisements, the screen displays in very large letters:

"THIS IS NOT A CINEMA,
THIS IS AN OPERA HOUSE,
A THEATRE", ETC.

These brief sentences accompanied by dazzling shots from amazing angles and ultra-loud three dimensional sound, of; Shakespearean plays, Puccini 's Operatic arias, Ballet-dancers, etc. All of these images advertising 'LIVE' performances from the best front-row seats in the best venues. My mind was buzzing, all that I had understood about the evolution of Film and Cinema had eventually culminated in this arena. I was actually experiencing real-live performances from real venues; great theatre, etc., and my thoughts switching back and forth between the adverts and some of the implicitly religious films I have written about from time to time; and the analytical side of my brain, now drawing conclusions from these trembling thoughts, among which, is that the evolution of cinema corresponded with the devolution of organised religion, perhaps not precisely but sufficiently enough to see that perhaps the human need for contact with the 'transcendent' now finds itself through the ultimate public medium of,'Not a Cinema'?

For in virtually occupying front-row seats that are not physically there, and experiencing the absence of performing bodies, (which are also mere chimera), as well as multi-directional digitalised Sound, downloaded from the internet, these resurrected images will touch us, but with what kind of magic?

The magic I have in mind is a special kind of magic, that dispels against all odds and against all earthly powers, the hegemony of empires and institutions, and against irrationality and illogicality, against the current tide of smart-alecy-atheism, against the stupidity of dedicated materialism; against all of these; there remains, for me, *signals of transcendence,* although the signals seem to be fading. But against the busy contradictory tide and flow and drawing out of daily life, there is still the small voice of calm that might catch us unawares. It might catch us at any odd moment, as a 'thief in the night'. Never-the-less it continues to come! Perhaps disguised as someone or something else; un-musically or as 'un-poetically', but it comes anyway, and lodges itself in our souls, leaving a small ache in the form of a 'word', or a 'song', or a 'shadow'; a persistent but not obvious signal, coming as disguised voices, or hidden messages; in the street or from a radio, mostly when we are half asleep! Of course it necessarily hides in symbols, in the shade of the garden or words of strangers and little children, but when it comes it can wound or worry us! It comes in many forms, most powerfully for me during the opening chorus of Mahler's Eighth Symphony, the 'Symphony of a Thousand', as in the Latin text of the ninth century Christian hymn for Pentecost: *'Veni, Creator Spiritus, mentes tuorum visita'* - 'Come Creator Spirit, visit the minds of your people!'

I am especially fussy when it comes to Coffee and Whisky, but I can take my poetry as is comes, not in words alone, especially not only in words, but literally anything that in any way speaks to my soul; for that is how I define poetry; as the *language of the soul.* I hear it, and see it, and think it, and feel it; I mention this only as a means of avoiding any misunderstanding, for I too frequently find myself in situations, where in making comments referring to 'poetry' or 'the poetical', causing a sudden stalling in conversations, a physical and psychological resistance, I notice in my respondents. (those I'm talking to or with).

This morning I intended continuing with writing my article on Freud, when the strangled sounds of Dire Straight's *'Money for Nothing'* fought their musical ways through the usual garbage piling-up and blocking the slender creative pathways between my synapses and my fore-finger, about to strike a button on the computer keyboard. When this happens there is always a tussle in my soul, between that actual real life moment, and the moment of a finger suspended in mid air, about to strike a particular computer key, and my *unconscious memory.* In this case the 'encapsulated memory' regenerated by muffled sounds from the radio, floated into my consciousness rendering my moving finger static, was Dire Straight's "Money for Nothing and Chicks for Free", a referent of the song sweating in the kitchen - he installing a fridge-freezer, ruminating on what it must be like to be a famous 'Rock Star'. There was a time when everybody else seemed to know about such things, especially my students. I heard their music but never listened to the words, until a few days after one particular Valentine's Day; but let the poetry speak for itself, not that I had the slighted idea where the poetry might take me!

I had just finished a psychology lecture to Student Nurses, most of them known to me, only in the sense that I saw them twice a week for a couple of terms, but still unable to put names to faces. As they filed out of the room that Valentine's Day, a pair of them stopped at the door, one of them too shy to speak, the other haranguing me for not sending the other, her buddy Jo, a Valentines card! It was a joke of course; I didn't know either of them to speak to, and although Jo was small, quiet and beautiful, I didn't give it another thought until several days later when a friendly female colleague in my Department, again jestingly referred to a particular student in her Eng-Lit class, who she claimed was 'ogling' me, for most the time during her lesson, from the window of her classroom; whilst I was teaching in the next classroom to her's. Again I let it go, but during the next week's lectures I sensed the girl's presence in the room and her attention. I sensed the danger to the point when the danger had already become part of the attraction, an imposing impossible attraction!

One afternoon she was waiting by my car in the college car park. I got into the car without speaking to her, opened the passenger door and she got in; again without a word spoken. The poetry was in the silence! We drove in silence, out of reach from the college, and pulled into a lay-by off the road. A redundant church was nearby, which she told me was haunted; she told me she was in love, I told her we were playing with fire! We walked through the overgrown churchyard, breathing it's ancient scents of rotting trees and green-dark moss; also what might have been mouldering traces of incense of holiness, or a swooning dopamine-saturated brains fighting for air? Miraculously in the bonding she had found her voice, asking me about my choice of music, giving me no time to reply; instead reciting poetical words I had never imagined; rhyming songs from Dire Straights and Elton John, and others I have forgotten. I didn't need to hear those words from anywhere else, I absorbed them through the pure or not so pure magic of her alchemy. 'Juliet when we made love you used to cry. You said I love you like the stars above, I'll love you till I die.'

Before this she had been the quietest student in the classroom, now she taught me all about poetry of 'Pop', and sang me lines from everything and everywhere, drawing me in to her magic circle. The following day, in college when we passed by one another, our eyes met; only our eyes; her face a mystery as if we had never, ever met! My days changed, my life changed. Sometimes in our lunch-times we stole away like secret lovers, to a country-side cafe for a Club sandwich; usually the only customers in the place! We survived like this until the end of the year, and into the start of her nursing training at a coast-bound hospital; I would drive late into the night to visit her. We both knew it was madness, that it wouldn't and couldn't last. We would sing our anthems and mouth our magic spells together; *"I guess that's why they call it the blues, time on my hands could be time spent with you, Laughing like children, living like lovers, Rolling like thunder under the covers, And I guess thats why they call it the Blues"*. I didn't need words to tell her it was poetry in any academic sense; had I attempted to, we both knew that the plain unpoetical words would be meaningless! This is no casual reminiscence, although it might be mistaken for one, nor is it even a love story, but instead, in the strange ways of Henry Corbin's,'*imaginal interruption*'; or in Bob Dylan's much simpler terms, distant 'Vision of Johanna'! 'The harmonicas play the skeleton keys, and the rains / And these visions of Johanna are now all that remains.' Or should I add: All I do is keep the beat and bad company. . . .!

But to those of the 'poetical,' merely 'keeping the beat' might appear to be too lackadaisically insufficient, in sustaining the life-blood of the poetical soul of humankind. Instead what is needed in an increasingly banal and soulless culture to recognise the one-time centrality of the poetical, or should I say the mythopoetic! To some extent this has already happened, as it does from time to time; but never quite enough to recover total belief in the 'oneness of the individual and the whole of mankind'. Instead what we have, is a cyclic historical trajectory of disenchantment, followed by re-enchantment and the rediscovery of the Supernatural that crossed the whole of Europe during the first half of the twentieth century. Besides the more popularised magical beliefs of everyday ordinary folk, a few intellectuals crossed international boundaries, met and gathered in the student quarters of the universities across Europe, mainly in the university student's Quarters and the new Cafe emporia of Austria and Germany, where poets, artists, intellectuals and philosophers and political revolutionaries met to share their ideas and beliefs. It was in the social and political turmoil of this period that like-minded individuals created their own versions of an alternative society!

One such gathering which grew into a free-thinker's commune, Ascona, on the gentle slopes of Monte Verita, the 'Hill of Truth', which began in 1900 when Henry Oedenkoven, a wayward son of a Dutch businessman, and his Girlfriend, bought a piece of land on the hillside by the shore of Lake Maggiore, to establish initially, a Vegetarian Colony, based loosely on the ideas of Jean-Jaques Rousseau and Henry-David Thoreau; attracting others who rejected conventional values of their societies, such as; capitalism, marriage, (holy wedlock!) private property, religious dogmas, eating meat and wearing clothes!

Their message was communicated via the Munich Schwabian meeting places, and the Viennese Cafes. Raphael Friedeberg, and anarchist physician arrived in Ascona, bringing with him other like-minded free-thinkers; writers, poets and artists and dancers, and other social dissidents, some of them already well known for their criticism of modernism. I had considered writing a list of the names of the pioneers at Monte Verita, but names alone would be insufficient to show the richness of talents and the off -beat thinking, about the invisible nature of reality, not only in the transcendence of individual imagining, but also as the expression of shared daily living, and making, and doing of each and all of them in that exciting alternative society; in communes dedicated to a New Society, at the start of the Twentieth Century, such as Monte Verita, and more recently in small-scale counter-culture groups, now scattered across the world.

The unsung heroes of Ascona I need to briefly consider to make my point, were:

Hermann Hesse, a Nobel Prize winner. Author of 'Steppenwolf,' a psychoanalytical and biographical study of Spiritual Crisis. And 'Siddarta', who found the meaning of Life and Existence. 'The Glass Bead Game', about a lifetimes learning to be able to play a Intellectual Game! Who after studying Latin, entered an Evangelical Seminary in preparation for becoming a Pastor, but was derailed by reading Nietzsche, Goethe, Schiller, and Greek mythology. Suffered from Depression and sought Freedom in Ascona.

And *Carl Jung*, the Swiss psychiatrist, who collaborated and argued with Freud over the over-emphasis of sexuality in child development, who went his own way, practicing psychotherapy and writing about the Collective Unconscious, Archetypes, Extroversion/Introversion, Synchronicity, Religious Belief, Mythology, Mysticism, Anthropology, Etc.

And *Erich Maria Remargue,* a German Novelist raised in a working-class Catholic family, who became famous with his Novel: "All Quiet on the Western Front", describing the agonising physical and psychological privations of Soldiering in the foul trenches on the Western Front, and the hypocracy of the military leaders.

Hugo Ball, German author and poet, and founder of the Dada Movement in European Art in Zurich; particularly the development of Sound Poetry - the bridge between musical composition and the phonetic quality of human speech. He came from a middle-class Catholic background, and gained recognition with his recording of his sound poem: Karawane, consisting of nonsensical words; the poetry existing in the resonances of sounds.

Else Lasker-Schuler, a Jewish German Poet., renown in Berlin for her exotic bohemian life-style, trained as an artist, but chose to express herself through Romantic and love poetry. A devotee of Expressionism, tried conventional married life with a Physician, but went her own way with several affairs. Attracted to the Free life style of Ascona; I love her short poem, An 'Old Tibetan Rug', which begins: 'Yoursoul, which liveth mine, is woven with it into a rug - Tibet. Strand by strand, enamoured coloures, Stars that courted each other across the length of heavens . . .

Stephan George, Symbolist Poet, and translator of Dante, Shakespear and Boudelair. Although homosexual, he famously courted the "Bohemian Countess" - *Fanny zu Reventlow*, and followed the French poets Paul Verlaine and Stephane Mallarme, and dreamt of making a new kingdom governed by intellectual and artistic elites. Described by his admirers as 'attractively priestly'; some of his poems set to music by *Arnold Schoenberg.*

Isadora Duncan, a French /American dancer, born in San Francisco to a poor family, but learned to dance at an early age by watching show-girls dancing, then earning money by giving dancing lessons to neighbourhood children in front room. Eventually travelling to New York, where her unique poetical style of dancing clashed with all other dancers, but sufficiently expressive for her to dance all over Europe; eventually taking Paris by storm with her exotic semi-nude dancing. She mixed with celebrities and the internationally famous, including the infamous occultist Aleister Crowley. Then returned to America, then to Russia, where she founded a Dancing School in Moscow. Most importantly she left her mark on all who saw her dance, as well as creating a philosophy of dance, tracing its early sacred roots back to ancient Greece. She moved all over the Mediterranean, eventually stopping-by The 'Hill of Truth', enjoying ultimate freedom to dance completely naked! Her death was as dramatic as her life; strangled by a precious hand-painted silk scarf, given to her by the Russian artist Roman Chatov. She is remembered as "The Mother of Dance"!

Carl Eugen Keel, was a little known Swiss Painter, who preferred working with basic materials, simple rustic woodcuts, and wrought-iron sculptures

Paul Klee, a Swiss-born artist from a musical family; his parents nurturing his musical talents, and expecting him to become a professional musician, but his own secret hopes were to become a painter. By the age of eleven he was already performing in public, but eventually he chose to study art at the Munich Academy of Fine Arts; excelling at Drawing. After graduating, he studied painting in Rome then back to Germany, sharing studios with other artists, drawing on the mixed influences of Expressionism, Cubism, and Surrealism, as well as developing his own personalised techniques, experimenting with various media, oil paint, watercolour, ink, glass, etc. His output of paintings and sketches exceeded 10,000 pictures, many exhibition pieces. He taught art and architecture at the Bauhaus, as well as his membership of "The Blue Rider' Russian Artists Group. His paintings had a fragile deep poetical quality.

Carlo Mense, a German Artist who enjoyed the company of other artis at Ascona, He described his own painting style as 'New Objective', meaning his use of basic shapes in clean-lines, bold colours, uncomplicated with the appeal of caricature. He taught art at several art schools, influencing post second WWII generations of artists.

Arnold Ehret, a German Naturopath, who helped Henry Oedenkoven found the 'Nature Life Colony' at Monte Verita, Ascona. Who after previously graduating in Art, was 'converted' to alternative medicine, leading to self experimenting with detoxification, fruitorinism, vitalism, and fasting. (He claimed that he once fasted for 105 days, with no ill effects!) After leaving the Monte Verita commune, he travelled to America to learn more about alternative remedies, and returning to Ascons, consequently opened his own Sanatarium there with his Nature -Health Cures. He appears, as a naked spindly-legged, bearded dancer, in several of the early 'Hill of Truth' photographs!

Rudolf Joseph Lorenz Steiner, was an Austrian philosopher and social reformer, and Founder of an esoteric spiritual movement - Anthropophy, which had its roots in German Idealist ideas, combined with comprehensible - practical approaches to spiritual beliefs including; education, medicine, agriculture, life-styles, etc., which Steiner regarded as essential aspects of his Philosophy of Freedom. Hence, his ideas and beliefs corresponded to the main features of Moute Verita's communal practices. He emphasised the importance of imagination, introspection, and intuition in children's education as the basis for a balanced individual's adult life, combining both the physical and spiritual dimensions of humans. His range of interests covered all aspect of human life, including town planning, architecture, food production, etc, which he related to individual's daily life; taking a phenomenological approach in his investigations. Whilst at the Monte Verita Commune, he shared his ideas with artists and other socially minded thinkers.

Mary Wigman, a German Dancer and Choreographer, was one of the most important figures in the history of modern dance. She took the dancing art to the highest levels with her graceful eurhythmics style, expressing music through her body movements. Her attendance at Monte Verita coincided with her growing interest in wider arcane issues, and the relationship between humans and the cosmos. She also came to see dance as a therapeutic activity. During her time at Ascona she broadened her approach to dancing to include poetical and artistic techniques.

Max Picard, a Swiss (Humanist) Author writing within the Platonic sensibility, on religious, political and psychological subjects. An indication of his interests can be gained from the title of his Novels: 'The Human Face', 'The Last Man', 'The Flight from God'.

Ernst Toller, a Left-Wing German Playwright, from a Jewish family, who drew on his own personal experiences as a Soldier in the Trenches on the 'Western Front' of the harsh physical conditions and the psychological impact of being bombarded continually weeks on end and expecting to die! After the War he was imprisoned for his (minor) participation in a revolution, including 149 days in solitary confinement. His Plays reflected the plight of powerlessness of individuals in repressive societies.

Henry van de Velde, a Belgian Painter, Architect and Interior Designer, who with two design partners, Founded Art Nouveau in Belgium, although he spent most of his Design career in Germany. Initially he opted for working as a Painter, but switched to General Design, including; fashion, furniture, interior-design, chinaware, cutlery. During periods at Monte Verita, he swapped ideas with other artists and writers, incorporating stylistic touches in his works

Fanny zu Reventlow, born into an aristocratic family, who had a difficult and disturbing childhood as a result of conflict with her mother; thrown out of Boarding school for arrogant behaviour, marrying to escape from her family, divorced after two years. Hanging out in the Cafes of Schwarbing, drawn to the intellectual elitism of the Munich Cosmic Circle by philosopher Ludwig Klages and the Mystic Alfred Schuler, which soon after, broke-up. She then moved onto the 'Munich Moderns' to be with the poet Rilke; eventually joining the artist at Monte Verita, where she wrote her 'Schwabing Novels', but needed to get married to share in an inheritance, which soon was lost after closure of the Bank! She was known as the 'Bohemian Countess of Schwabing', and survived by scrounging. She left Ascona, finding it difficult fitting-in!

Rudolf von Laban, famous as a pioneer of Modern Dance, born in Hungary, from French Nobility with its own bizarre history, invented his 'Laban Movement Analysis';

(a method of visualising, interpreting, and documenting human physical movement) for dance-performers and as therapy. He also constructed a Philosophy of Dance based on esoteric principles from; theosophy, Sufism, and fin de siecle Hermeticism, which established him as a central figure at Monte Verita, where among other activities he directed the stunning 'The Song of the Sun' on the Ticino hillside, celebrating the dawn! Whilst at Monte Verita he befriended Carl Jung and Joseph Pilates, - (inventor of the Pilates method of physical health).

Otto Gross, an Austrian Psychoanalist, who fought a private war with Freud, who mixed with the intelligentsia of Monte Verita Community, who described him as a 'brilliant-mind', influenced by the writings of Max Stirner, Peter Kropotkin, Franz Kafka, Nietzche, and the Berlin Dadaists. Became a drug-addicted Neo-Paganist come Proto-Feminist, and who seduced D.H. Lawence's wife Frieda von Richofen, poisoned another ex-lover, championed sexual liberation, contributed to Freudian psyochanalytic theory, and wrote a mind boggling book on the Soul! He acquired his drug habit from his South American patients whilst he Practiced Medicine, as a Naval Doctor working in the Tropics.

Erich Muhsam, -a German- Jewish Antimilitarist - Anarchist - Essayist, Poet, Playwright, Revolutionist, and Cabaret Performer, (think of Lotte Leya and Mack the Knife!) Who as a student, reported the brutality of his school-teachers, leading to a Court-case and dismissal. At university he started a course on Pharmacy but abandoned it to pursue his literary and poetical ambitions, which even his own father 'threatened to beat out of him.' He joined a like-minded group called the 'Neue Gemeinschaft' (New Society), which combined Socialist Philosophy, and Theology and Communal Living, became involved in 'Worker's Councils' (Soviets) and Workers Communes. Arrested and imprisoned several times, published revolutionary poetry and short stories, fled to Monte Verita to regain his strength, and returned like a refreshed fighter; finally to be arrested by the Nazi's as a: Communist, a Socialist, and an Anarchist. Tortured and Branded with a Swastika on his shaven scalp with a red hot branding-iron and executed by Storm Troopers, but recognised by the Ascona Community as a Martyr. The Titles of his Plays, including 'The Con Men', 'All Hang', 'Reason of State. His poems; 'Die Werte', Der Revoluzzer', 'Waste - Krater - Wolken.

Karl Wilhelm Diefenbach was one of the Founding Fathers of Monte Verita, with Henry Oedenkoven, and previously part of a smaller experimental commune at Himmelhof in Uber Sankt near Vienna, which he used as a model for Ascona. He was symbolist painter and deeply committed to building an Alternative Society where there was no Private Property, no Monogamy, no Religion, no Eating of Animals! He grew up in Hadamar, famous for its Clinic for Forensic Psychiatry, which ironically responsible for euthanasia of mentally retarded children during the Third Reich.

Walter Segal, born in Berlin, a son of a Romanian Jewish Artist, spent the whole of his adolescence during the First World War, living in the Monte Verita commune, that he regarded as his High-School education! After which, he studied architecture Berlin and Delft - Netherlands, and commissioned by his father to design and build, 'a small holiday cabin' in Ascona. Eventually he was able to combine both his formal architectural training and his Ascona experiences as part of his Design style. He moved to Highgate London, designingApartments in Knighsbridge, and the Animal buildings for Surrey Docks Farm. His legacy is the Legal Centre for Alternative Technology, contributing to developments in Healthy Living Homes.

Max Weber stayed at Monte Verita several times partly for Health reasons, but mainly for its opportunities for him to experience the joys of becoming part of a remarkable coterie of free-thinkers, including the English novelist D.H. Lawrence, and the glamorous von Richthofen sisters, Frieda and Else, daughter of Baron von Richthofen. All I had learned about Max Weber from my student days was that he had been *the* most important German Sociologist and social theorist, but nothing of the man himself; no interesting anecdotes, only so-called facts. I discovered the part he played in the 'life; of 'Hill of Truth' only when I read Martin Greens book 'The von Richthofen Sisters', sub-titled 'The Triumph and the'Tragic Modes of Love', which untangled Max Weber's love affair with Else, who had married Edgar Jaffe, a protege of Max Weber's. Her sister Frieda had married a British Language professor, who took her to Nottingham where he taught Philology, and where she fell in love with one of her husbands students, D.H.Lawence, with whom she eloped to Germany. In the intervening years, both sisters had affairs with Otto Gross, a sometime resident of Ascona, who fathered children with both sisters, both babies born at the same time, in 1907, and both given the identical name - Peter. Besides all of this, (as if not sufficiently bizarre) Max Weber experienced a complete volte-face after suffering a mental breakdown, leaving him unable to work or write for five years, but regained his health after several periods spent at Monte Verita.

As Joachim Radau explains in his excellent Biography 'Max Weber' (2005): "Weber found everything at Ascona on Monte Verita he needed to regain his health; Vegetarianism, nudism, free love, ecstatic dance, Oriental esotericism: all were jumbled together, partly in intimate association, but also in painful tension with one another." The painful tension referred to the psychological difficulties Weber experienced coming to terms with his life-changes, and his discovery of his new found self and soul, which re-shaped the rest of his life, and his approach to his sociological theorising and writing. For example, during the time he was researching material for his 'Protestant ethic book, he befriended an amateur philosopher - Graf Keyserling, whose ideas on 'the body' now corresponded to Webers 'new outlook' on life, but grated with Marianne, his un-reborn wife's stolid attitudes. She wrote to Else to tell her that Max was being assisted in his research by, 'one of th strangest creatures she had ever met: "A spiritual nomad and wanderer, who channels all the religions and civilisations and possibilities through his mind . . . The man speaks so fast that at first I can't understand him at all, still less follow what he says - it was altogether exciting, this cyclone that beat you about the ears with China, Confucius, Japan, India, Buddha, Brahman (sic!), theosophy and god knows what else. He was here for three hours a day, speaking incessantly, laughing and clapping whenever Max said something he liked. . . In short, he struck me as severe, a little foolish - but very likeable in a childlike way . . . It is incredible that with this oddly voracious and talkative nature he really lives alone for nine months of the year - and *keeps silent*. But somehow this metamorphosing into a thousand shapes, from Indian holy man to Manchu prince and then Japanese and an American, seemed to me a little terrifying." It would seem to me that this 'nomadic wanderer' would have provided a cool blast of fresh air for both Max and his wife, if only they had taken the gist of his words seriously.

Throughout his life Weber knew there were contradictions in his personality. He sought help from Freud for his depressive condition, who put it down to a combination of 'impotence and masocism', but which Max and his wife Marianne believed was caused by the stress of overwork; described as 'the iron cage', and later in life as 'demons', Which were excised through his love for Else Richthofen and declared in a love letter: 'I am yours' - although once again, beloved mistress, you can say to me and of me, 'You are mine', in the most daring senses. . . Because I know from the dark years - ah yes! That you and you alone have the power to condemn me to humiliation and torment if you so wish it . . . Therefore, even if you were not infinitely superior to me in each and every respect, I would still be in your thrall. . . Believe me, I know that even everything that plunged me into uncertain darkness came from the best of you, which is holy to me - from a sense of responsibility and from the chivalrousness of your love, you wondrous child of the gods.'

This, from the man described by his intellectual peers as; 'The foremost social theorist of the twentieth century, the principal architect of modern social science.', as well as one of Ascona's favourite sons! Yet what emerged from Ascona was not dependent on any one singular contributor, especially when considering the intellectual and aesthetic range and the cross-pollination of all the combined talents and ideas; from the shared consciousnesses and their collaboration, that with hindsight I would describe as Akasha (from the Sanskrit) which fed-back to the Ascona group, which in turn led to a programme of 'Yearly Lectures' from 1933 up to the present; superbly celebrated in Hans Thomas Hakl's book titled 'ERONOS', *an alternative intellectual history of the twentieth century,* (2013). Described as the Chronicle of the Eronos Meetings -(named after the Greek word for *banquet)* where guests bring their (intellectual and aesthetic) food; constituting one of the most important gatherings of international scholars and influential thinkers in the twentieth century, including; Carl Jung, Erich Neumann, Mircia Eliade, Martin Buber, Walter Otto, Paul Tillich, Gershom Scholem, Herbert Read, Joseph Campbell, Karl Kereyni, D.T. Suzuki, Adolf Portman, et al.

And Erwin Schrodinger, Archetypal Bohemian, brilliant mathematician, Nobel Prize-winning Physicist, Romantic poet, Lover of beautiful women, self-proclaimed Roue, Inventor of Wave-Mechanics Theory, Follower of the Vedanta; very much a Man larger than life! Whose semi-permanent 'menage et trois life-style' conflicted with the administrators of Princeton and Oxford universities. From early in his career he had the keenest sense of his own particular strengths; looking back on his life some years after he had gained celebrity status, he reflected: "In my scientific work (and moreover also in my not so private life) I never followed one main line, one program defining a direction for a long time. Although I can work only poorly in collaboration, and unfortunately all not with my pupils, my work in this respect is still not entirely independent, since if I am to have an interest in question, others must also have one. My word is seldom the first, but often the second, and may be inspired by a desire to contradict or to correct, but the consequent extension may turn out to be more important than the correction, which served only as a connection."

At the peak of his career, in which he was collaborating with other leading theoretical physicists; Heisenberg, Dirac, Bohr, Pauli, and Einstein, he was frequently in disagreement with the others, but drawing on his own broader philosophical inclinations, he would point out that scientific data '*does not alone represent the natural object in itself, but rather the relation between subject and object.*' Schrodinger's strength was in his own understanding of life as being 'all of one piece'; his scientific interests, philosophy of Schopenhaur whose works included Buddhism, the Vedanta, and the Christian Mystics, his Romantic poetry, and romantic attachments; all together had considerable influence on Schrodinger, especially Schopenhauer's writings, which he studied in detail and came to absorb into his own understanding, reinterpreting them to reflect his spiritual needs.

He later wrote:

"Nirvana is a state of pure blissful knowledge . . . It has nothing to do with the individual. The ego or its separation is an illusion. Indeed in a certain sense two 'I's are identical, namely, when one regards all their special content - their *Karma*. The goal of man is to preserve his Karma and to develop it further. The goal of a woman is similar but somewhat different: namely, so to speak, to create an abode that accepts the Karma of man . . . When a man dies, his Karma lives and creates for itself another carrier." This idea of Karma is not orthodox Hinduism, but his own interpretation to fit in with the rest of his Lifeworld; his romantic relations with women, and his poetry; most of the time a combination of both. For example, His 'Lovesong', a poem he wrote to Sheila May Greene in Dublin; 'No one knows as you and I / How with us it came to be. /Not a ones there to see / When we kissed so fervently. No one knows / That heaven loves us so / That is gives us everything / That how to give it knows. And whoever might see us / Would scarcely think / The in wide space / Of all else void. Are we alone, only we / And all our joy / Never never do I return / Except with thee.' Whilst in love with one particular woman the moment, his passions totally consumed him, but like a willow-the-wisp he could suddenly be consumed by another. It was the same with his theorising, a new idea would enter his thinking, and he would be off, like a whippet chasing a hare, in my mind the sure sign of a mystic! This happened soon after Sheila announced that she was pregnant, which at first delighted him; but he had been taken by another prettier face!

His romantic excursions in Dublin coincided with new developments in field theory, and the renewal of his correspondence with Einstein after a hiatus of more than two years. Einstein sent him two unpublished papers: "I am sending them to nobody else, because you are the only person known to me who is not wearing blinkers in regard to the fundamental questions in our science." This exchange of ideas with Einstein led to Schrodinger's first paper on 'The General Affine Field Laws', delivering lectures in Dublin, Cambridge and Zurich, and from there back to Ascona to take part in an 'Eronos Tagung' (conference), with the topic: 'The Spirit of Science'. He spoke on the 'true relation of spirit (Geist) to science, quoting Sankara's commentary on the Vedanta-sutras: 'Subject and object - the "I" and the "not - I" - are in their essence opposed to each other like light and darkness.' The great Indian philosophers were concerned only with the 'Ego that consists of thought' and it's relation to the Godhead. Schrodinger wished to identify this Ego that consists of nonself, and the 'spirit, strictly speaking, can never be the object of scientific inquiry, because objective knowledge of the spirit is a contradiction in terms. Yet on the other hand, all knowledge relates to the spirit, or more properly, exists in it, and this is the sole reason for our interest in any field of knowledge whatsoever.'

He was making the point that scientific study can never give us any understanding of the nature of the Spirit. And that it would be a false thing that even the most exact knowledge of biophysics, physiology, or psychology can ever cause us to regard the spirit as something constrained or 'mechanically determined' by scientific principles." In spiritual matters of the soul, any knowledge we acquire, instead of being systematic like that of ordinary subjects, is 'picked up' mainly through anecdotes, which at first seem to be isolated gobbets, that eventually somehow become connected and interconnected, creating an awareness that we seem to have known all of our lives. After completing his final papers on Unified Field Theory, Schrodinger spent more time on his poetry and philosophy; publishing a book of his poetry, including his meditation on 'waking early in the morning': "In those short twilight nights / When the sun greets you in the north / And day flows into day and light to light / To near entwine themselves in one long day - You forget almost the swan of hellish powers /A flux of self destruction in your life / And once again believe the pure and the lawful / Words from which salvation springs. Yet now alas the days decline / And silent winter chills your boundless longing / As darkness casts its shadow on your soul. Thus all its ardent striving turns to farce. / With nothing left it but had stifled scorn / Even as it struggles toward annihilation."

A new and wider understanding of human consciousness emerged from Schrodinger's 'Unified Field Theory', contributing to 'debates' on consciousness, human memory and spirituality. Debates that eventually entered the public domain leading to broader questions on; ecology and climate change, healthy eating, our relationship with nature and animals, human identity, nurturing the Human Soul! Schrodinger read books on Buddhism, Samkhya and Yoga, Vedanta, the Religion of Ancient India, as well as what he learned from others at Ascona, especially Carl Jung. My own approach in this has been go directly to the source or translations of the original sources; to study; The Rig Veda, The Bhagavad Gita, The Mahabharata, and the Upanishads, and read and think about 'Subtle Bodies'.

Recently I was treated by a young Indian Doctor in my local A&E. Far too young I thought, to know about the Vedas. But nevertheless I asked her if she knew anything about subtle bodies. Her face immediately lit-up. We discussed Atman and Western concepts of the soul; our private discussion was part of my treatment; I soon felt a lot better! In Sanskrit there is no History and no Tragedy; no Herodotus or Thucydides; and no Aeschylus or Sophocles or Euripides as in Western philosophy; on the other hand there are hundreds of anecdotes, and three-hundred old prayers for Brahman and Atman. These are two names of 'One Truth' and the two are One and the same. The Truth of the Universe is Brahman; our own inner Truth is Atman. The Sacred OM is a name for both Brahman and Atman. One of the meanings of OM is Yes! If we ask where is Brahman, the Spirit of the Universe, we must look in the Upanishads:- "He is seen in nature in the wonder of a flash of lightning. He comes to the Soul in the wonder of a flash of Vision." In one of my other books, "The Homely Mind of Multiple Realities", I touch on 'Field Theory', which attempts to explain how a new Consciousness Paradigm operates; actually not in our heads as I once believed, but as a vast 'Invisible Field Force' across the whole universe, as described by Dr. Larry Dossey in his book 'One Mind'; (an excellent Reader on the subject, if anyone needs a starting point), in looking backwards and forwards, from the ancient Akashic Field to Quantum Mechanics; including the idea of entanglement and nonlocality, which is one of the more unusual features of quantum mechanics which states; that for distant particles to demonstrate nonlocal connections and entanglement, they must have previously been in direct contact; which would have been the case for all matter/energy at the point of the Big Bang, as well as the fusing of 'poetry and physics', as defined by Gerald Manley Hopkins in his poem, 'Nature is a Heraclitean Fire . .!

Considering the range and depth of scholarship in philosophy, history, art and science, and its exploration of mystical and religious symbolism in 'Eranos' (2013) and the high academic status of its contributors, it is surprising that so little interests has been shown by mainstream academia or the media. I take this apparent lack of interest as an true indicator of the spiritual health of western civilisation! Despite the concentrated efforts of the scholars of religion; psychologists, philosophers, physicists and biologists for nearly sixty years, the best we can say is, that they kept the beat; 'aiming to serve the life that exists within the mesocosm [the intermediary spiritual world between the macrocosm and the microcosm]. Through their exploration of archaic traditions of thought and forms of harmony, between rational and non rational experience, and varieties of the inner spiritual realms and how modern generations might tap into the things that have the power to make us whole, things which we are in dire danger of losing!

In Steven Wasserstrom's 'Religion After Religion'(1999), he focuses on three of Eronos's scholars of religion; Mythologist - Mircea Eliade, Judaist - Gershom Scholem, and Islamist - Henry Corbin; each of them influenced by Jung's theory of archetypes in one way or another, all three leaders in their field and regular Lecturers at Eronos. Between the three of them they created a platform of ideas with its emphasis on the centrality of the mystical experience, myth, gnosis, esoterism and eschatology, drawing on Boehme's 'theosophy', Schelling's 'theogonic process', Nietzsche's 'beyond good and evil', Jung's 'archetypes', and Rudolf Otto's 'idea of the holy'. But each with his own 'take'! Their works were highly academic; aimed at those with a 'professional' interest in religion; attractive to philosophers, theologians - (especially theologians), sociologists and thoughtful clergy; but there are insights, crumbs for the common man! Between them they projected their combined view of the autonomous reality of the "imaginal," the "sacred," and "religious reality," underpinning their vision of Religion after religion. As Sholem put it; "We wished to immerse ourselves in the study of the finest detail. We were seized by a compulsion to deal with the dry details, the small things of the great things, so as to develop therein the closed well of turbulent vitality, for we knew that this was its place and there it was hidden, and that from there could draw upon its waters and quench our thirst. We sought the great scientific ideas which would illuminate the details, like the rays of the sun playing upon the surface of the water, yet we knew — and is there any serious man of science who has not experienced this eternal debate within his heart? —that it does not dwell in the details themselves . . . And we thereby became specialists, masters of one trade. And if we did not struggle with God, as in the words of the *Haggadah*, we struggled with the Satan who danced among us. This was the Satan of irresponsible dilettantism, who does not know the secret of construction, because he does not know the secret of destruction."

Steven Wasserstrom offers no explanation for his choice of the book's title; Religion after Religion (1999), to have done so would have been contradictory to his purpose, which is to explore many of the tacit assumptions that have informed the study of religious culture in our time. He does this through the intelligent use of anecdotes for the chapter headings. Where he leads I will follow!

"The historian of religions is in a better position than anyone else to promote the knowledge of symbols, his documents being at once more comprehensive than those at the disposal of the psychologist or the literary critic; they are drawn from the very sources of symbolical thinking. It is in the history of religions that we meet the "archetypes," of which only proximate variants are dealt with by psychologists and literary critics." — *Mircea Eliade.*

Only the poet has re-integrated the world that in the rest disintegrates.—*Rainer Maria Rilke.*

"The word *esoterism*, so often misused, refers to the unavoidable necessity of expressing the reintegration of the human being in symbols." *HenryCorbin.*

"The aim of every symbol: the reintegration of man into the All" . . *Mircea Eliade.*

"I am that I am" said the God of Abraham. Only some such divine tautology would seem to do justice to us all: the old woman who sees ultimate meaning in her grandchild, the mathematician who sees it in a formula, the tribesman who see it in a crocodile. The meaning of life is that it should mean. At everyday levels surely meaning is one with nourishment. — *James Merrill.*

"Perhaps the most important function of religious symbolism —especially important for the role it will play in later philosophical speculation — is its capacity for expressing paradoxical situations to certain patterns of ultimate reality that can be expressed in no other way." —*Mircea Eliade.*

"The keynote of [mysticism] is invariably a reconciliation . . .of the opposites of the world, whose contradictoriness and conflict make all our difficulties and troubles." *William James.*

"Only in Europe. . . has the human mind dared to act in a way that assumes incompatibles." — *Denis de Rougemont*

"As for the symbol, it is characterised by the fusion of two contraries, the great and the particular, or to use Schelling's favourite formula, by the fact that the symbol does no simply signify, but also is . . ." *Tzvetan Todorov*

"I am an unsymbolic thing. My meaning is what I am. You turn the ring in vain. I have no sense." *Paul Klee*

"On the gates of this theology I would inscribe the profound words of Johann Georg Hamann, 'Language is the mother of reason and revelation." *Gershom Scholem.*

"It is beginning to be realised that the rediscovery of symbolism's perhaps the most important discovery of our age." *Mircea Eliade.*

"But the attempts to discover the hidden life beneath the external shapes of reality and to make visible that abyss in which the symbolic nature of all that exists reveals itself: this attempt is as important for us today as it was for those ancient mystics." — *Geshom Scholem*

"Ascona's legacy was new uses of the imagination."— *Martin Green.*

"Is not the position of the spiritual hermeneutic . . . similar to that of the artist?" — *Henry Corbin.*

"I came to bring fire! How I wish it were blazing already." *St. Luke,12:49-53*

"Everything created is worth being liquidated!"— *Johann Goethe's Mephisto*

"The first stage of our regeneration is our recall from the land of oblivion or kingdom of death and darkness, for this is indispensable for our entrance into the path of life." — *Louis-Claude de Saint-Matin*

"In such moments of total crisis, only one hope seems to offer any issue — the hope of beginning life over again. This means, in short, that the man undergoing such a crisis dreams of new, regenerated life, fully realised and significant." — *Mircea Eliade*

"Counter-history is ultimately more true than history". — *Henry Cobin*

"And perhaps it wasn't so much the key that was missing, but the courage: courage to venture out into an abyss, which one day could end up in us ourselves, courage also to penetrate through the symbolic plain and through the wall of history."— *Gershom Scholem.*

"I am still waiting for an apocalyptic angel with a key to the abyss". — *J.G. Hamann, cited by Martin Heidegger*

"We are all of us, and *Evans* first of all, would-have-been believers; we are all religious spirits without religion." — *Emil Cioran*

"We came as rebels and found ourselves to be heirs."— *Gershom Scholem.*

"For example, there was a man at this ferry who was my predecessor and teacher. He was a holy man who for many years believed only in the river and nothing else. He noticed that the river's voice spoke to him.He learned from it; it educated and taught him. The river seemed like a god to him and for many years did not know that every wind, every cloud, every bird, every beetle is equally divine and knows and can teach just as well as the esteemed river. But when this holy man went off into the woods, he knew everything; he knew more than you and I, without teachers, without books, just because he believed in the river." — Siddartha, (HermannHesse)

To return to that other mode from another time, not Jo, but Suzanne who takes me down to her place near the river. Where I hear the boats go by, and spend the night beside her, and I know she's half crazy, but that's why I want to be there, and she feeds me tea and oranges, that come all the way from China. And just when I mean to tell her, she gets me on her wavelength and, she lets the river answer: 'That I've always been her lover!'. But Suzanne was more than half crazy, she thought I could cure her madness. Like the Irish girl who once knew me, who was dying of disappointment, not getting her promotion, in the job she never wanted, shot-full of electrotherapy that sent her even madder, who told me secretly of a visit, by the Blessed Virgin Mary, who gave a magic Rosary, that she thought would have cured her, but her condition was circumstantial, she told me, 'if you touch me', she'd be well! The same with Maria Rilke, whose works which were mystical and haunting, who fell beneath the spell of Lou Andreas - Salome, not the one in Herod's story, but the one who psychoanalysed him, made him flee to Russia, on the 'Rolling Ocean of the Volga, dedicating his Book of Hours, to God his loving neighbour, telling Him of his anguish, of his love for Lou-Andres, how the madness sneaked-upon her, how his Faith had made him famous, knowing Pasternack and Tolstoy, his epiphanic magic power leading to transcendence, finding

God everywhere - everything, even in the tiniest little thing! But beyond this rhyming there was Eronos, its Alternative Intellectual History, of the twisted Twentieth Century. Hallelujah, Amen!

The older I get the longer the days! Which now start at four in the morning when the bedroom is still in total darkness and gradually brightening as the sun comes up. It is during this time of thirty or so minutes, that I am visited by several members of my family, who seem to have chosen this time for their 'visitation' during which we sometimes share small intimacies. Not simply memories, but new reflections and meditations on the tiniest inconsequential occurrences from our lives long ago. By four-thirty my mind is racing madly, buoyed-up by our brief reunion in bardo; reviewing other ideas floating around in my mind and how I might attempt to explain them, in what I will write during the rest of the morning. By eight o'clock I am fully awake, and might listen briefly to the BBC News, most of which I dismiss as transitory and beyond my immediate concern and interest But I recall one morning back in 2017, listening to the news I heard a brief comment, among all the other news-gibberish, that an American writer had won the Man Booker Prize, for his Novel 'Lincoln in Bardo'. Now that was my kind of News; not because the winner was an American, but because his title suggested to me that my own occasional morning reunions' were not so weird after all! Later I discovered that the novel had been based on a true story of the death of eleven year old 'Willie Lincoln', the American President Lincoln's son, who had died of typhoid fever. The novel opens in Bardo, which is an intermediary state between life and the afterlife, where young 'Willie' Lincoln materialises in the Bardo, meeting other souls of those who have recently died. Grief-stricken, the boy's father visits the mausoleum for consolation and to say a prayer, but when he is about to leave he finds himself 'pulled back' finding himself in conversation with his son, who tells him of his new discoveries in the afterworld.